P9-CLJ-948

Do you like to pretend that you are someone from long ago? Find out more about people and their stories at:
www.harcourtschool.com/hss

Reflections

CALIFORNIA SERIES

People We Know

Harcourt
SCHOOL PUBLISHERS

Orlando   Austin   New York   San Diego   Toronto   London

Visit *The Learning Site!* www.harcourtschool.com

MAPQUEST®

TIME® FOR KIDS

HARCOURT SCHOOL PUBLISHERS

Reflections
PEOPLE WE KNOW

Senior Author

Dr. Priscilla H. Porter
Professor Emeritus
School of Education
California State University, Dominguez Hills
Center for History–Social Science Education
Carson, California

Series Authors

Dr. Michael J. Berson
Associate Professor
Social Science Education
University of South Florida
Tampa, Florida

Dr. Margaret Hill
History–Social Science Coordinator
San Bernardino County Superintendent of Schools
Director, Schools of California Online Resources for
  Education: History–Social Science
San Bernardino, California

Dr. Tyrone C. Howard
Assistant Professor
UCLA Graduate School of Education & Information Studies
University of California at Los Angeles
Los Angeles, California

Dr. Bruce E. Larson
Associate Professor
Social Science Education/Secondary Education
Woodring College of Education
Western Washington University
Bellingham, Washington

Dr. Julio Moreno
Assistant Professor
Department of History
University of San Francisco
San Francisco, California

Series Consultants

Martha Berner
Consulting Teacher
Cajon Valley Union School District
San Diego County, California

Dr. James Charkins
Professor of Economics
California State University
San Bernardino, California
Executive Director of California Council on Economic
  Education

Rhoda Coleman
K–12 Reading Consultant Lecturer
California State University, Dominguez Hills
Carson, California

Dr. Robert Kumamoto
Professor
History Department
San Jose State University
San Jose, California

Carlos Lossada
Co-Director Professional Development Specialist
UCLA History–Geography Project
University of California, Los Angeles
Regional Coordinator, California Geographic Alliance
Los Angeles, California

Dr. Tanis Thorne
Director of Native Studies
Lecturer in History
Department of History
University of California, Irvine
Irvine, California

Rebecca Valbuena
Los Angeles County Teacher of the Year—2004–05
Language Development Specialist
Stanton Elementary School
Glendora Unified School District
Glendora, California

Dr. Phillip VanFossen
Associate Professor, Social Studies Education
Associate Director, Purdue Center for Economic Education
Department of Curriculum
Purdue University
West Lafayette, Indiana

Content Reviewer

Dr. Judson Grenier
Professor of History Emeritus
California State University, Dominguez Hills
Carson, California

Classroom Reviewers and Contributors

Roswitha Mueller
Teacher
Tahoe Elementary School
Sacramento, California

Jeannee L. Schlumpf
Teacher
J.H. McGaugh Elementary School
Seal Beach, California

Christine M. Steigelman, M.A. Ed.
Teacher
Manzanita Elementary School
Newbury Park, California

Loreta V. Torres
Teacher
Fairmount Elementary School
San Francisco, California

Melinda Trefzger
Teacher
William Northrup Elementary School
Alhambra, California

María Villa
28th Street Elementary School
Los Angeles, California

Karen Westbrook
Teacher
Sage Canyon School
San Diego, California

Maps
researched and prepared by

Readers
written and designed by

Requests for permission to make copies of any part of the work should be mailed to:

School Permissions and Copyrights
Harcourt, Inc.
6277 Sea Harbor Drive
Orlando, Florida 32887-6777
Fax: 407-345-2418

Acknowledgments appear in the back of this book.

Printed in the United States of America

ISBN 0-15-338499-9

2 3 4 5 6 7 8 9 10 032 15 14 13 12 11 10 09 08 07 06 05

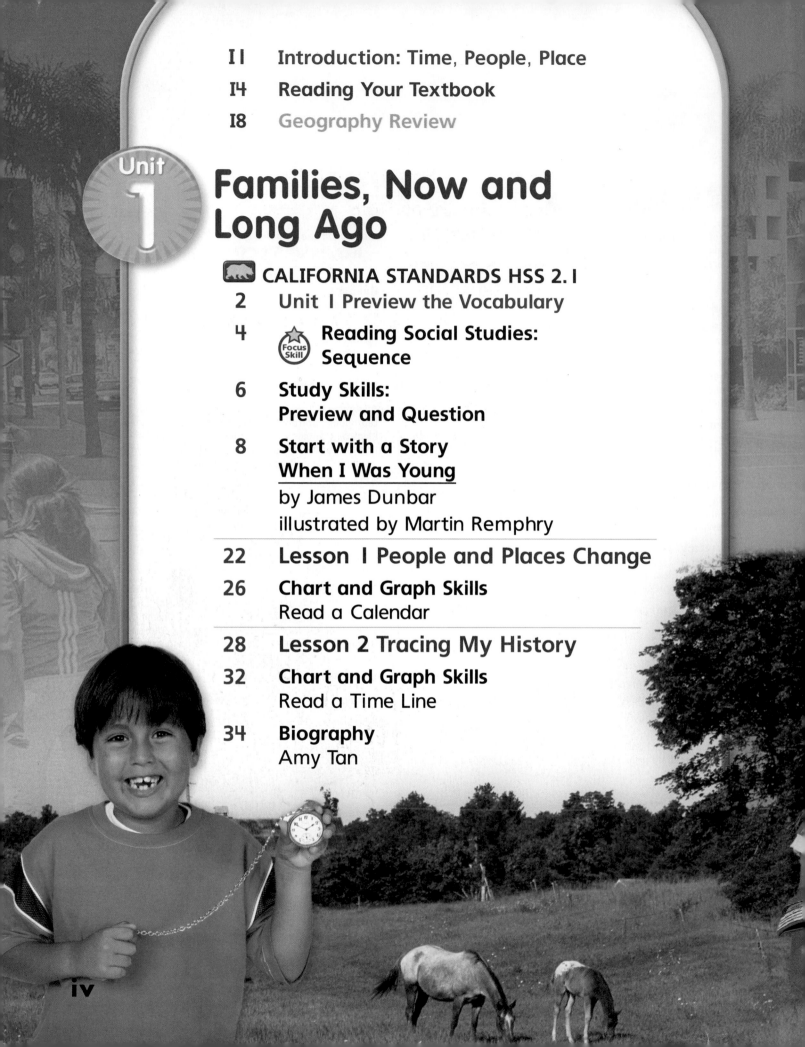

Unit 1

Families, Now and Long Ago

🐻 **CALIFORNIA STANDARDS HSS 2.1**

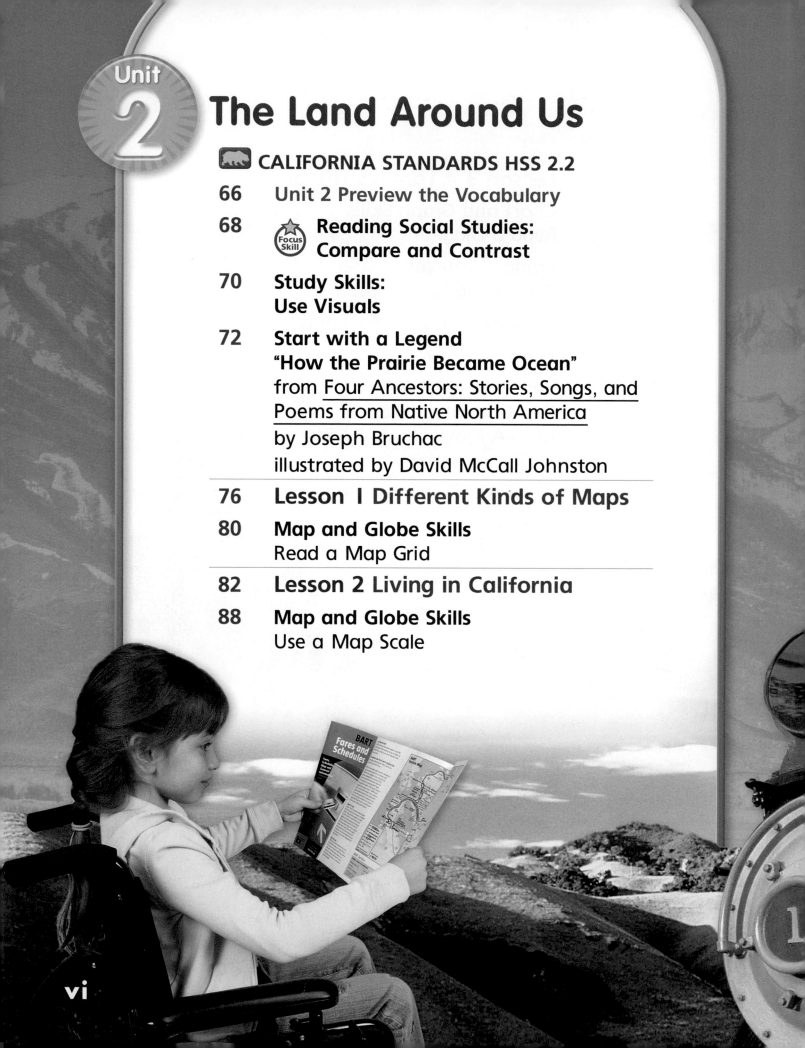

Unit 2

The Land Around Us

CALIFORNIA STANDARDS HSS 2.2

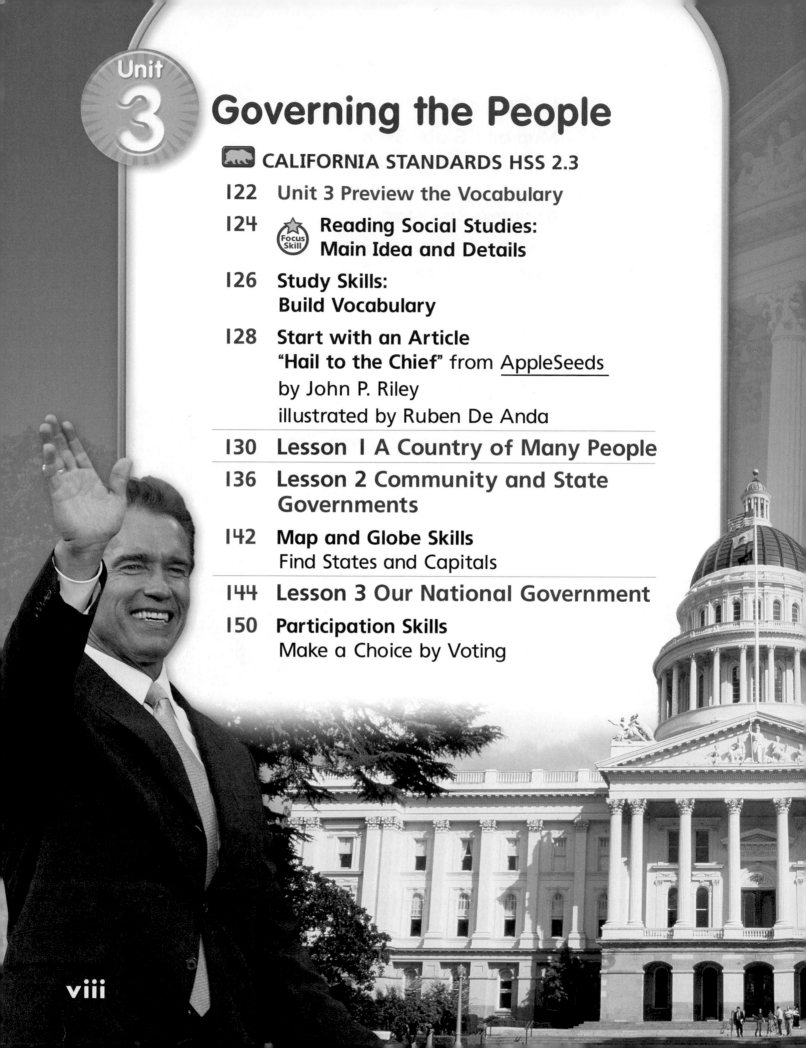

Unit 3

Governing the People

CALIFORNIA STANDARDS HSS 2.3

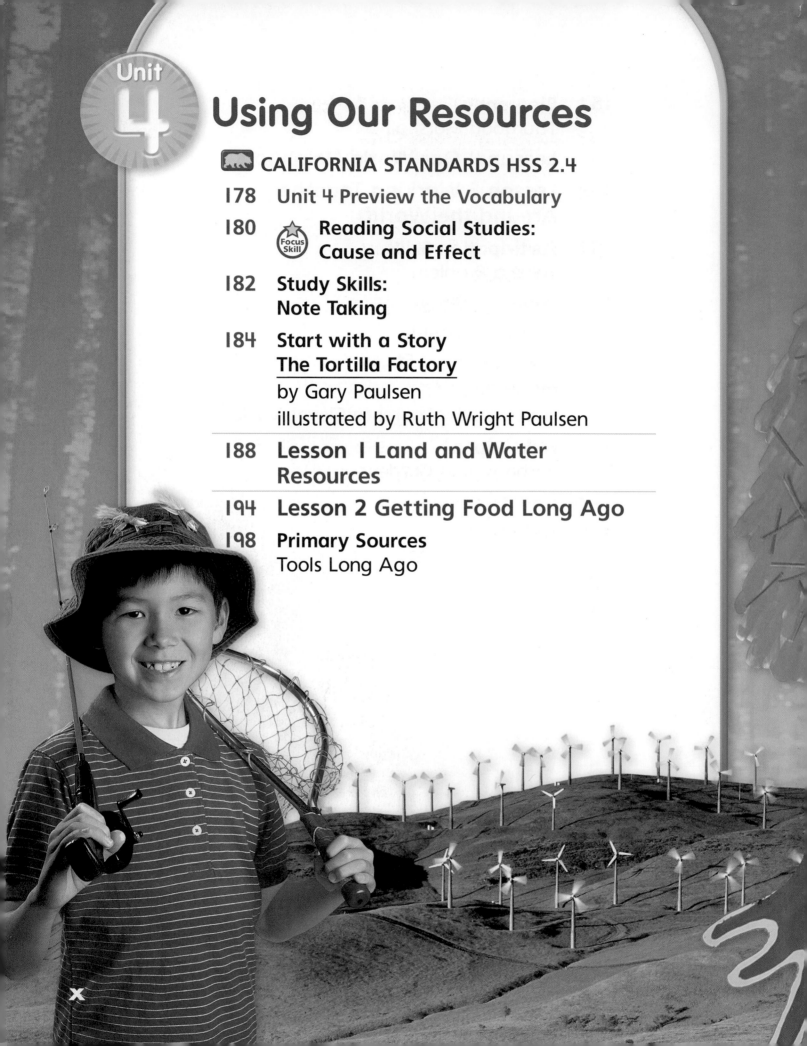

Unit 4

Using Our Resources

CALIFORNIA STANDARDS HSS 2.4

Unit 5

People in the Marketplace

CALIFORNIA STANDARDS HSS 2.4

Unit 6

People Make a Difference

xiv

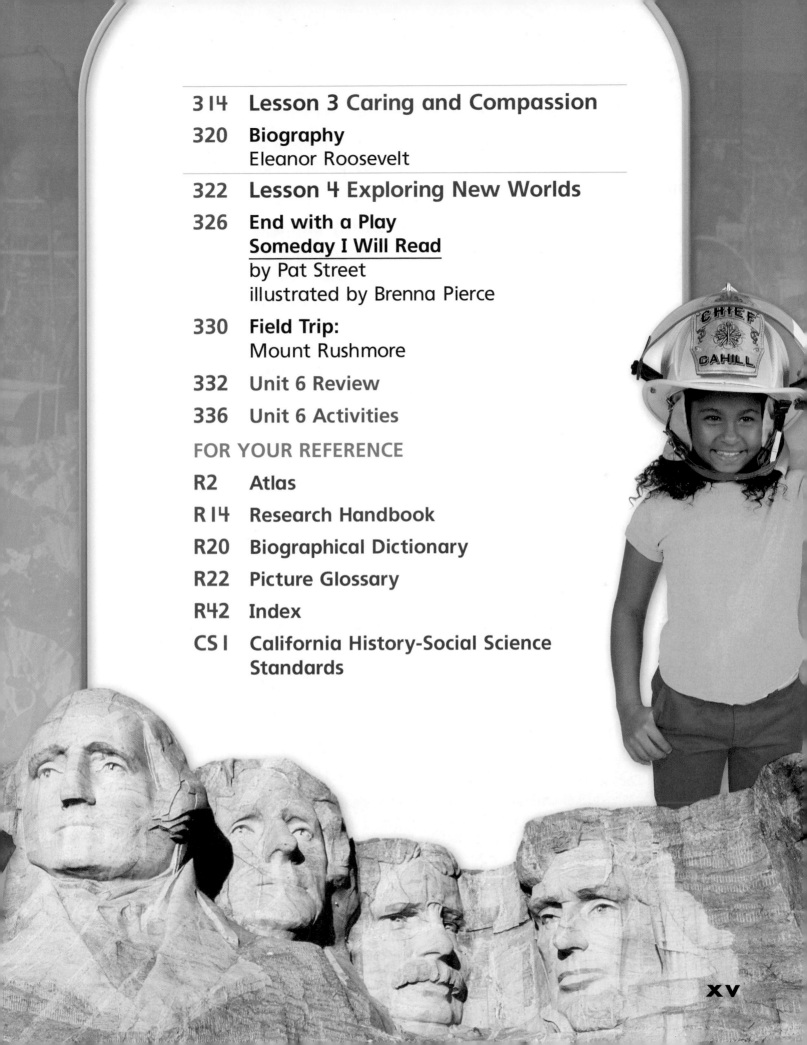

xv

Features

Skills

Chart and Graph Skills

Participation Skills

Map and Globe Skills

Critical Thinking Skills

Reading Social Studies

Study Skills

Citizenship

Points of View

Literature and Music

Primary Sources

Documents

Biography

Geography

Cultural Heritage

Children in History

A Closer Look

Field Trips

Charts, Graphs, and Diagrams

Maps

Time Lines

The Story Well Told

"I wanted children now to understand more about the beginnings of things. . .what it is that made America as they know it."

Laura Ingalls Wilder in Laura Ingalls Wilder: A Biography

by W. Anderson

Do you ever wonder about people who lived in a different time or place? This year you will be learning about how families have changed over **time**. You will meet special **people** who we remember for the important work they have done. Also, you will visit **places** near and far to see where people live and how they use the land around them.

People We Know

You can learn how people lived long ago by reading the story of a family's past.

Important people teach us how to behave.

We get most of our food
from the land.

Reading Your Textbook

GETTING STARTED

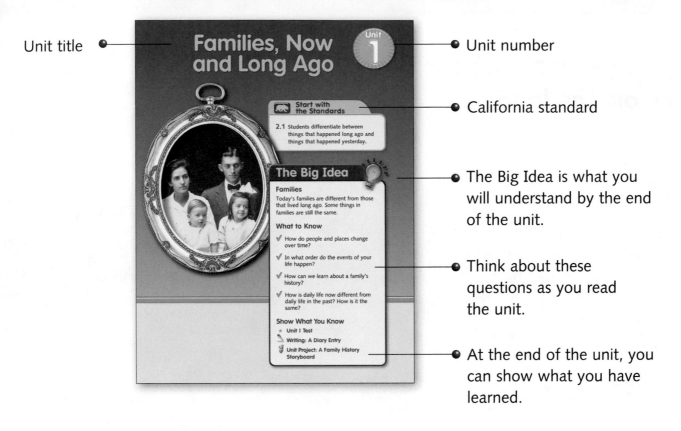

Unit title

Unit number

California standard

The Big Idea is what you will understand by the end of the unit.

Think about these questions as you read the unit.

At the end of the unit, you can show what you have learned.

PREVIEW VOCABULARY

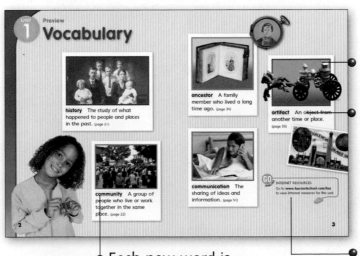

A photograph helps you understand the meaning of the word.

The definition tells you what the word means. The page number tells you where to find the word in this unit.

Each new word is highlighted in yellow.

The unit has more information and activities on the website.

READING SOCIAL STUDIES

Reading skill and explanation

Model paragraph for reading practice

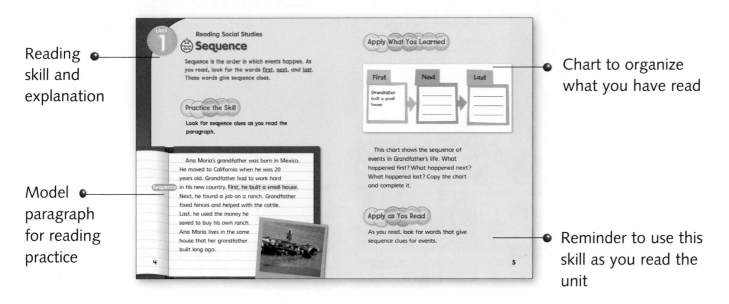

Chart to organize what you have read

Reminder to use this skill as you read the unit

STUDY SKILLS

Study skill and explanation

Activity to practice study skill

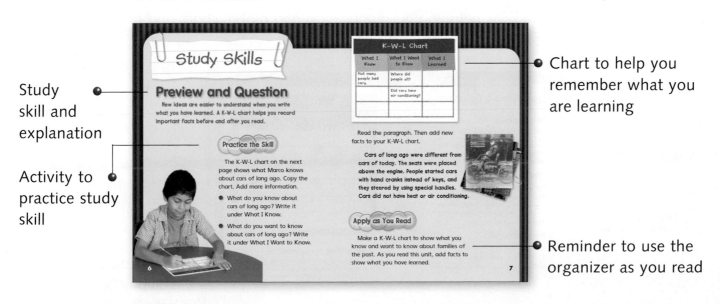

Chart to help you remember what you are learning

Reminder to use the organizer as you read

READING A LESSON

Lesson number

Guiding question

Some main ideas to find

New words to learn

Reminder to use your reading skill

California standards

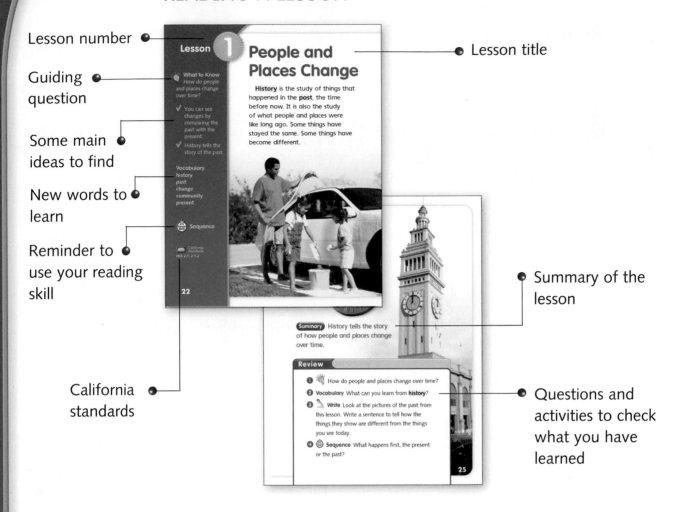

Lesson title

Summary of the lesson

Questions and activities to check what you have learned

PRACTICING SKILLS

Skill lessons help you build your map and globe, chart and graph, critical thinking, and participation skills.

Skill category
Skill lesson title

Why the skill is important

Skill practice questions

Independent skill practice activity

SPECIAL FEATURES

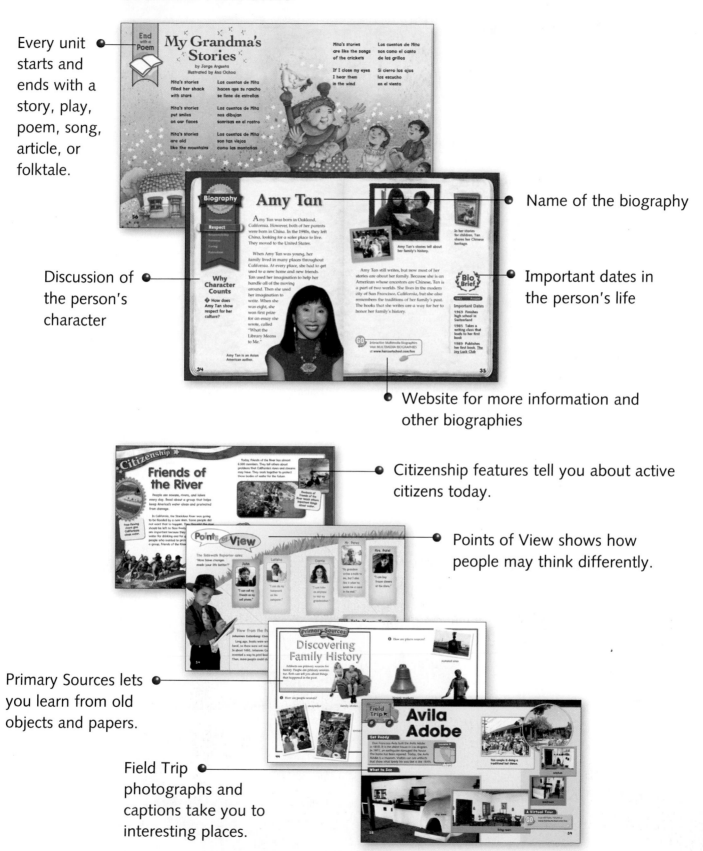

Every unit starts and ends with a story, play, poem, song, article, or folktale.

Discussion of the person's character

Name of the biography

Important dates in the person's life

Website for more information and other biographies

Citizenship features tell you about active citizens today.

Points of View shows how people may think differently.

Primary Sources lets you learn from old objects and papers.

Field Trip photographs and captions take you to interesting places.

Go to the Reference section in the back of this book to see other special features.

The Five Themes of Geography

The story of people is also the story of where they live. When scientists talk about the earth, they think about five themes or main ideas.

Location

Everything on Earth has its own place.

Place

Every location has features that make it different from other locations.

GEOGRAPHY

Human-Environment Interactions

People can change the environment or find ways to fit into their surroundings.

Movement

Each day, people in different parts of our state and country and around the world trade goods and ideas.

THEMES

Regions

Areas of Earth that share features that make them different from other areas are called regions.

Looking at Earth

The true shape of Earth is shown best by a globe. A **globe** is a round ball. It is a model of our planet. With a globe, you can only look at half of Earth at one time. You can spin the globe to see the other half.

On a map of the world you can see all the land and water at once. A **map** is a flat drawing that shows where places are. This map of the world shows the seven continents. A **continent** is one of the seven main land areas on Earth. It also shows that much of the world is covered by large areas of water called **oceans**.

ANALYSIS SKILL Name the seven continents and four oceans you see on the map.

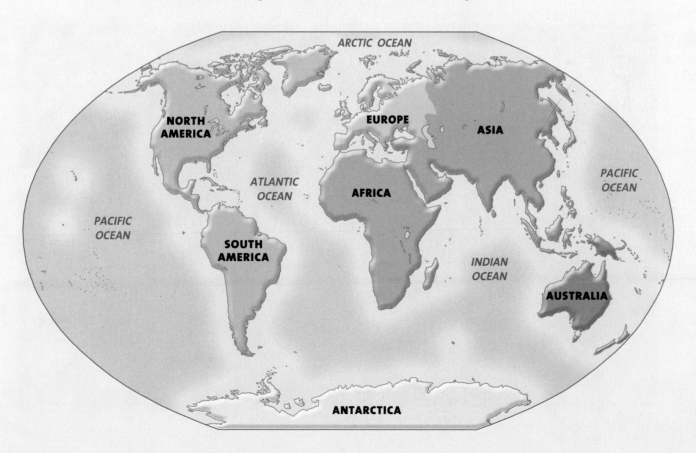

View from Above

Does your neighborhood have a school, a grocery store, a library, a fire station, a park, and a bank? These are places that people share in a neighborhood. You can learn about a neighborhood by looking at a photograph.

You can also learn about a neighborhood by looking at a map. Mapmakers use photographs taken from above to draw maps. They draw symbols to help you find places on the map. A **map symbol** is a small picture or shape that stands for a real thing.

ANALYSIS SKILL **How is this map like the photograph? How is it different?**

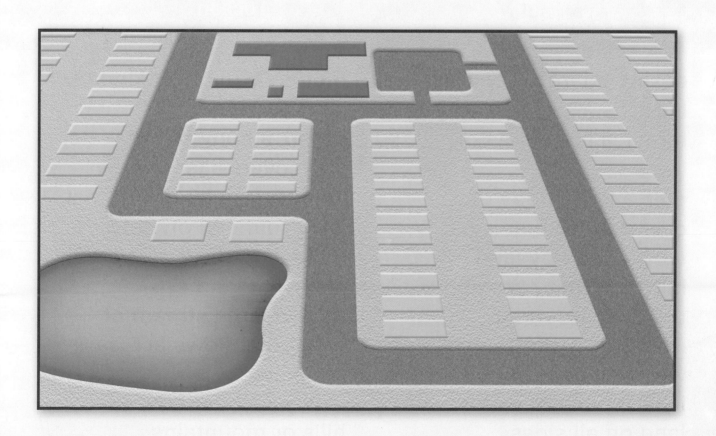

Geography Terms

mountain

lake

valley

river

forest

plain

hill

desert

gulf

island

peninsula

ocean

desert a large, dry area of land

forest a large area of trees

gulf a large body of ocean water that is partly surrounded by land

hill land that rises above the land around it

island a landform with water all around it

lake a body of water with land on all sides

mountain highest kind of land

ocean a body of salt water that covers a large area

peninsula a landform that is surrounded on only three sides by water

plain flat land

river a large stream of water that flows across the land

valley low land between hills or mountains

114

Families, Now and Long Ago

 Start with the Standards

2.1 Students differentiate between things that happened long ago and things that happened yesterday.

The Big Idea

Families

Today's families are different from those that lived long ago. Some things in families are still the same.

What to Know

✔ How do people and places change over time?

✔ In what order do the events of your life happen?

✔ How can we learn about a family's history?

✔ How is daily life now different from daily life in the past? How is it the same?

Show What You Know

★ Unit I Test

✎ Writing: A Diary Entry

✐ Unit Project: A Family History Storyboard

Families, Now and Long Ago

1874

1914

Talk About
Families

" The names of family members from long ago are written in our family Bible."

1933

1950

1971

2007

"My great-great-grandfather carried this watch from Mexico."

"My mother and grandmother played with this doll."

Vocabulary

history   The study of what happened to people and places in the past. (page 22)

community   A group of people who live or work together in the same place. (page 24)

ancestor   A family member who lived a long time ago. (page 36)

artifact   An object from another time or place. (page 37)

communication   The sharing of ideas and information. (page 52)

GO ONLINE

INTERNET RESOURCES
Go to **www.harcourtschool.com/hss** to view Internet resources for this unit.

Reading Social Studies

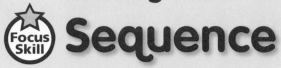

Focus Skill — Sequence

Sequence is the order in which events happen. As you read, look for the words <u>first</u>, <u>next</u>, and <u>last</u>. These words give sequence clues.

Practice the Skill

Look for sequence clues as you read the paragraph.

 **Sequence**

Ana Maria's grandfather was born in Mexico. He moved to California when he was 20 years old. Grandfather had to work hard in his new country. First, he built a small house. Next, he found a job on a ranch. Grandfather fixed fences and helped with the cattle. Last, he used the money he saved to buy his own ranch. Ana Maria lives in the same house that her grandfather built long ago.

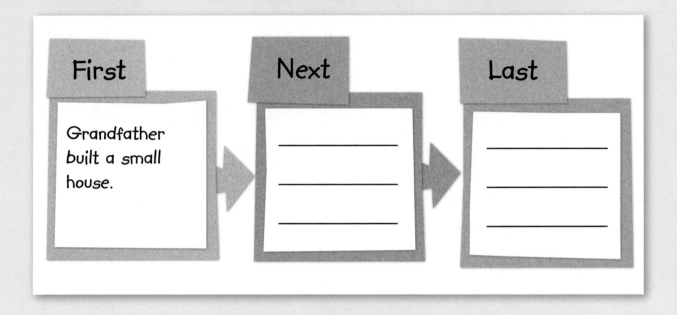

First	Next	Last
Grandfather built a small house.	_____ _____ _____	_____ _____ _____

This chart shows the sequence of events in Grandfather's life. What happened first? What happened next? What happened last? Copy the chart and complete it.

Apply as You Read

As you read, look for words that give sequence clues for events.

Study Skills

Preview and Question

New ideas are easier to understand when you write what you have learned. A K-W-L chart helps you record important facts before and after you read.

Practice the Skill

The K-W-L chart on the next page shows what Marco knows about cars of long ago. Copy the chart. Add more information.

● What do you know about cars of long ago? Write it under What I Know.

● What do you want to know about cars of long ago? Write it under What I Want to Know.

K-W-L Chart

What I Know	What I Want to Know	What I Learned
Not many people had cars.	Where did people sit?	
	Did cars have air conditioning?	

Read the paragraph. Then add new facts to your K-W-L chart.

Cars of long ago were different from cars of today. The seats were placed above the engine. People started cars with hand cranks instead of keys, and they steered by using special handles. Cars did not have heat or air conditioning.

Apply as You Read

Make a K-W-L chart to show what you know and want to know about families of the past. As you read this unit, add facts to show what you have learned.

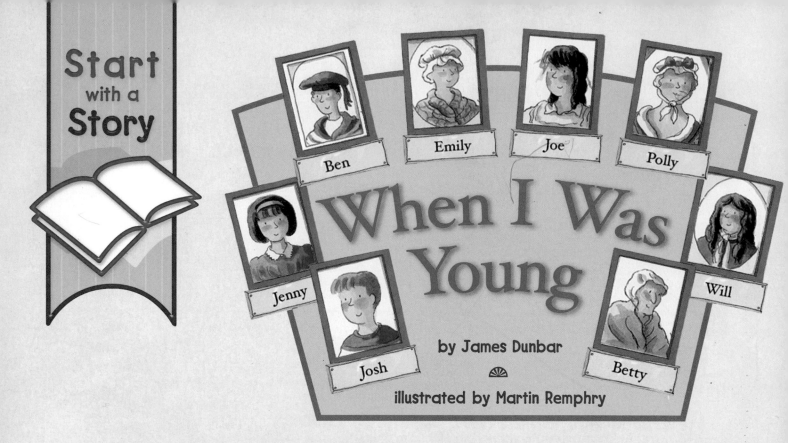

Ben

Emily

Joe

Polly

Jenny

When I Was Young

Will

Josh

by James Dunbar

illustrated by Martin Remphry

Betty

Josh likes visiting Grandma Jenny.
Her apartment is full of her memories.

"What was it like when you were
young, Grandma?" asks Josh.

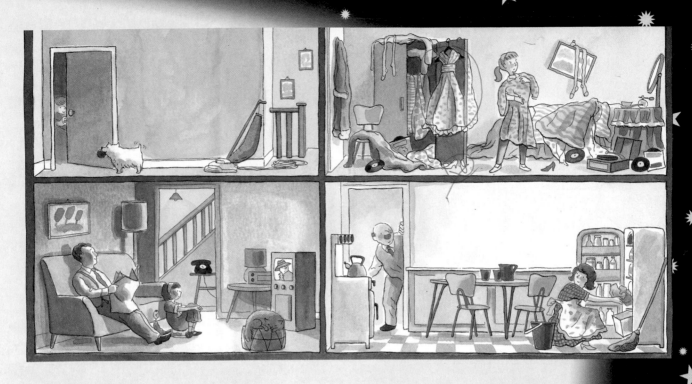

And Grandma Jenny says—

When I was young, we lived in a new house and got our first TV. We had a kitchen with an electric stove and a fridge. Grandpa Ben used to visit us on weekends. My sister used to dress up and go dancing every Saturday night.

9

I remember asking Grandpa
what it was like when he was
young. And Grandpa Ben said—

When I was young, in England, my mum
and dad worked in a big hotel. Dad used
to polish the carriages. Sometimes he let me
feed the horses. I saw a car in the street
for the first time.

I remember the first time we had our photo taken. This is me in my sailor suit with mum, dad, my brother, Ted, my sister, May, Grandpa Jim, and Grandma Emily.

I asked Grandma Emily what it was like when she was young. Grandma Emily sat me on her knee and said—

When I was young, I remember playing in the street with all the other children. At night, I used to get scrubbed in a bathtub in the kitchen. We had candles for lighting.

We lived in a busy town. Grandfather Joe used to take me to the docks. We watched the big ships from all around the world come and go.

13

I used to ask Grandfather what it was like when he was young. Grandfather Joe sat me on his knee and said—

When I was young, I lived in the country. My father and grandfather worked on a farm.

At harvesttime everybody helped, even my Grandmother Polly.

Two days each week, we went to the
village school. The teacher was very strict.

I remember asking my grandmother what it was like when she was young. Grandmother Polly sat me on her knee and said—

When I was young, I used to help my older sister, who worked at a big house. Downstairs in the kitchen, I polished candlesticks and scrubbed the tables and helped prepare the food. Upstairs in the large rooms, I dusted the furniture and helped make the fire.

I remember the fair coming to town. There were games and dancing and market stalls.

I used to ask my grandfather what it was like when he was young. Grandfather Will sat me on his knee and said—

When I was young, we traveled to all the country markets where my father and grandfather bought and sold horses.

18

I remember Grandmother Betty making dolls and small
toys. They were made from wood. I used to help paint the
faces. She gave one of the wooden dolls to me . . .

I remember thinking, "When I am as old as Grandmother Betty, I will tell my grandchildren what it was like when I was young."

Betty
Born in 1648

Will
7 years old in 1697

Polly
7 years old in 1744

Joe
7 years old in 1796

Jenny
7 years old in 1952

Emily
7 years old in 1848

Josh

Ben
7 years old in 1899

Response Corner

Make It Relevant Find out what life was like for an older relative when he or she was your age.

What to Know
How do people and places change over time?

✔ You can see changes by comparing the past with the present.

✔ History tells the story of the past.

Vocabulary
history
past
change
community
present

 Focus Skill Sequence

 California Standards
HSS 2.1, 2.1.2

People and Places Change

History is the study of things that happened in the **past**, the time before now. It is also the study of what people and places were like long ago. Some things have stayed the same. Some things have become different.

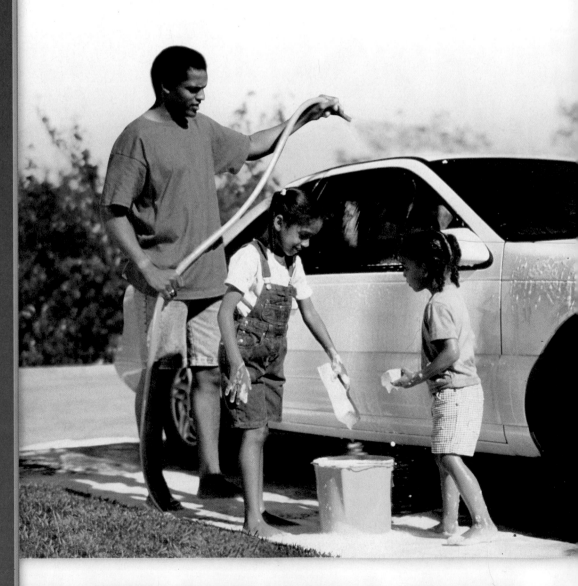

A **change** happens when something becomes different. The homes people live in, the clothes they wear, and the ways they have fun all change. These things are different now from the way they were long ago.

Past, 1920s

Past, 1920s

Communities change, too. A **community** is a place where people live and work together.

Long ago, your community looked different. Over time, new houses and roads were built. Look around your community. You can see what it looks like now, in the **present**.

ANALYSIS SKILL Which photograph shows the past? Which photograph shows the present?

Long ago, people kept track of time by using shadows, grains of sand, drops of water, and candles.

Summary History tells the story of how people and places change over time.

Review

1. 💡 How do people and places change over time?

2. **Vocabulary** What can you learn from **history**?

3. ✏️ **Write** Look at the pictures of the past from this lesson. Write a sentence to tell how the things they show are different from the things you see today.

4. ⭐(Focus Skill) **Sequence** What happens first, the present or the past?

25

Read a Calendar

❯ Why It Matters

To find out what time of day it is, you need a clock. To find out about days, weeks, or months, you need a calendar. A **calendar** is a chart that keeps track of the days in a week, month, or year.

❯ What You Need to Know

1 There are seven days in a week.

2 There are about four weeks in a month. Most months have 30 or 31 days. February has just 28 days or, in some years, 29 days.

3 There are 12 months in a year.

❯ Practice the Skill

1 How many days are in this month?

2 What day of the week is September 15?

3 What is going to happen on September 24?

September

Sunday	Monday	Tuesday	Wednesday	Thursday	Friday	Saturday
						1
2 Christa McAuliffe	3 Labor Day	4 School Begins	5	6	7 Grandma Moses	8
9	10	11	12	13 Art Class	14	15
16	17	18 Computer Class	19	20	21	22
23	24 Guest Speaker	25	26	27	28 Music Class	29
30						

❯ Apply What You Learned

Make It Relevant   Make a calendar page for next month. Show events that will happen at school. Show any other important days to remember.

Tracing My History

We shared our histories in class. I made a storyboard. A **storyboard** uses words and pictures to show important events. An **event** is something that happens. I put the events in order from first to last.

I was born in El Paso, Texas.

28

The first picture shows me when I was a baby. The second picture is of San Diego, the city my family moved to. The next picture shows me on the day I lost my first tooth.

Rico Peralta

We moved to San Diego, California.

I lost my first tooth.

The last picture shows me going to visit my grandmother in Mexico. We had a big family reunion while I was there. I met uncles, aunts, and cousins I had never seen before. I was happy to share my storyboard with my class.

I took my first airplane trip.

Cultural Heritage

Family Reunions

As families grow, some members move away. They may telephone, write letters, or e-mail. They also come to family reunions to join in the fun and celebrate their history.

Summary A storyboard can be used to show important events in order.

Review

1. 🔆 In what order do the events of your life happen?

2. **Vocabulary** What kinds of events can be shown on a **storyboard**?

3. ✏️ **Write** Make a storyboard about events in your life. Use the storyboard to write your autobiography, or the story of your life.

4. ⭐ **Sequence** How do you know which picture to place last on a storyboard?

Read a Time Line

❱ Why It Matters

You can measure minutes and hours with a watch. You can measure days, weeks, and months with a calendar. A **time line** tells you when things happened. It can cover a long time or a short time.

❱ What You Need to Know

You read a time line from left to right. The earliest events are on the left. This time line covers ten years. A mark shows the start of every year.

2000   2001   2002   2003   2004   2005

I was born in Compton, California.

We had a party on my fifth birthday.

▶ Practice the Skill

A time line is like a storyboard. It shows important events. It also shows the years in which the events happened.

1 When was Shelly born?

2 Did Shelly get a dog before or after her fifth birthday?

3 When did Shelly move to Long Beach?

▶ Apply What You Learned

ANALYSIS SKILL **Make It Relevant**   Make a time line of events in your life.

2006   2007   2008   2009   2010

We got our first dog, Daisy.

We moved to Long Beach, California.

Trustworthiness

Respect

Responsibility

Fairness

Caring

Patriotism

Why Character Counts

❓ **How does Amy Tan show respect for her culture?**

Amy Tan is an Asian American author.

Amy Tan

Amy Tan was born in Oakland, California. However, both of her parents were born in China. In the 1940s, they left China, looking for a safer place to live. They moved to the United States.

When Amy Tan was young, her family lived in many places throughout California. At every place, she had to get used to a new home and new friends. Tan used her imagination to help her handle all of the moving around. Then she used her imagination to write. When she was eight, she won first prize for an essay she wrote, called "What the Library Means to Me."

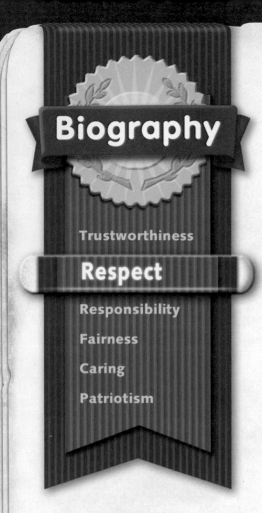

In her stories for children, Tan shares her Chinese heritage.

Amy Tan's stories tell about her family's history.

Amy Tan still writes, but now most of her stories are about her family. Because she is an American whose ancestors are Chinese, Tan is a part of two worlds. She lives in the modern city of San Francisco, California, but she also remembers the traditions of her family's past. The books that she writes are a way for her to honor her family's history.

GO ONLINE Interactive Multimedia Biographies Visit MULTIMEDIA BIOGRAPHIES at **www.harcourtschool.com/hss**

Bio Brief

1952   **Present**

Important Dates

1969 Finishes high school in Switzerland

1985 Takes a writing class that leads to her first book

1989 Publishes her first book, The Joy Luck Club

A Family's History

What to Know
How can we learn about a family's history?

✔ Every family has its own history.

✔ Many sources tell about a family's past.

Vocabulary
ancestor
artifact
source
heritage

 Sequence

California Standards
HSS 2.1.1

"Tell me about my family." Lan Nguyen loves to listen to her mother's stories about their family's history.

"Your **ancestors** are your family members who were born long before you. They lived in Vietnam. Your father and I were born in Vietnam, too," Mother says.

"Vietnam is a big country in Asia. Your father and I didn't know each other when we lived there. We met here, in California, after moving to the United States."

Mother has an old box filled with **artifacts**, or objects from the past. She says, "These artifacts belong to our family. They are a **source** for learning about our family's history."

Inside the box are a fan, coins, a set of paints, and a flute. Mother takes out the flute. "My father played this flute for us every night. He taught me how to play." She plays a song on the flute. "That song is part of our family's heritage. **Heritage** is something that is passed down from your ancestors."

Mother says, "I was your age when I moved to the United States. This was my favorite dress. I wore it when I moved here." Lan dances with the dress while Mother plays another song.

Mother opens the family scrapbook. It is filled with clippings and photographs.

Lan reads a news story about Father's art. Some of his paintings hang in Lan's house. "Your father was happy to share his painting," Mother says.

"What are these photographs about?" Lan asks.

"They show the first Tet celebration we took you to," Mother says.

October 2, 1999

Local & State

Local Artist's Art on Display

Tran Nguyen's painting will hang at the university during the month of October.

Tet 2003

"Tell me more about our history," Lan says. She wants to hear all of Mother's stories.

Summary We can learn about a family's history from many sources.

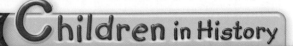

Children in History

Vietnamese Boat People

After a long war in Vietnam, some of the people there did not feel safe. They wanted to leave, but they were not allowed to go. Some people left in secret. Many of these were children. They hid with their families in small, crowded boats. They sailed for days, feeling afraid, but hoping to come to a safe place.

Review

1. How can we learn about a family's history?

2. **Vocabulary** What are some kinds of **artifacts**?

3. **Activity** Interview a family member. Ask him or her to tell you a family story.

4. **Sequence** Are your ancestors people who lived before you or people who will live after you?

Read a Diagram

❯ Why It Matters

A **diagram** is a picture. It shows the parts of something. A family tree is a kind of diagram. It shows the parts of a family. It can tell you about a family's history.

What You Need to Know

This family tree tells about Lan Nguyen's family. It tells about Lan, her parents, and her grandparents.

Practice the Skill

1 Where can you find the youngest people on a family tree diagram?

2 Who are the people on the middle row of this family tree?

3 What are the names of Lan's grandparents?

Apply What You Learned

Make It Relevant Make a family tree that tells about your family.

Discovering Family History

Artifacts are primary sources for history. People are primary sources, too. Both can tell you about things that happened in the past.

family stories

1 How are people sources?

storyteller

reenactor

44

2 How are places sources?

restored sites

historic markers

statues

❸ How are artifacts sources?

special objects

newspapers

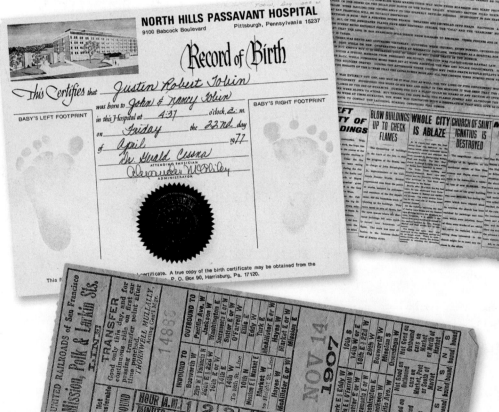

certificates

tickets from important events

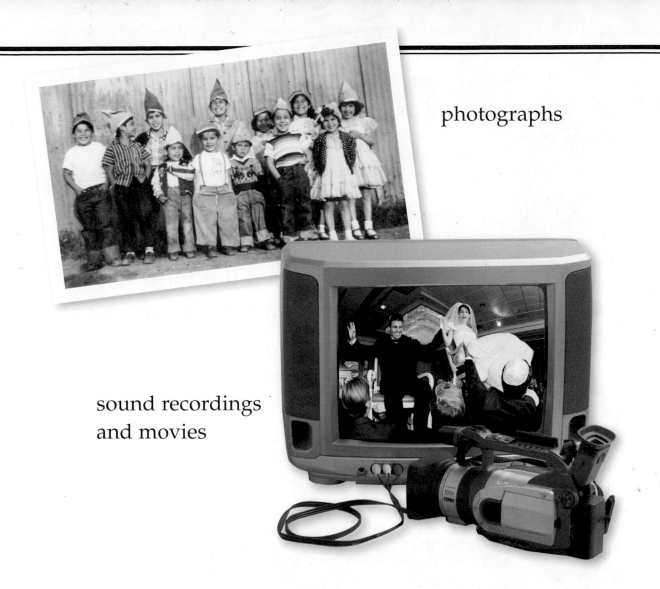

photographs

sound recordings
and movies

![ANALYSIS SKILL] **Analyze Primary Sources**

Make It Relevant   Find out three things about
your family's or community's history. Use different
sources for each—a person, a place, and an artifact.

GO ONLINE   Visit PRIMARY SOURCES at
www.harcourtschool.com/hss

4

Daily Life Then and Now

What to Know

How is daily life now different from daily life in the past? How is it the same?

✓ Daily life changes over time.

✓ Traditions link the present to the past.

Vocabulary
transportation
tradition
communication

Focus Skill Sequence

California Standards
HSS 2.1, 2.1.2

Bobby Dodd lives on a farm. His family has owned the farm for many years. Bobby lives in an old house and plays in a big barn that once held many horses.

Long ago, horses did many jobs on farms. They pulled plows up and down the fields. Horses were also used for transportation. **Transportation** is the moving of goods and people from place to place. Horses pulled wagons to town. They also pulled buggies to take people where they wanted to go.

Today, Bobby's father plows with a tractor. A bus takes Bobby to and from school. There are now paved roads instead of the dirt tracks of long ago.

Long ago, Bobby's ancestors pumped water by hand and used candles for light. Shade trees cooled the big house. People cooked food on a stove that burned wood.

Now Bobby just turns a faucet to get water. The house has electricity for light, for cool air, and for cooking.

Every year, Bobby's family has a big cookout. It is a **tradition**, or a way of doing something that is passed on in families. At the cookout, friends and family have fun doing some things people did long ago, such as playing horseshoes, dancing, and making homemade ice cream.

Tradition is important to Liz Fong's family. Her ancestors moved to California from China long ago. Liz's grandmother taught her the tradition of calligraphy. In this kind of writing, Liz uses a brush to form Chinese characters.

Sometimes Liz uses her computer to send e-mail to her friends. Writing and e-mails are kinds of communication. **Communication** is the sharing of ideas and information.

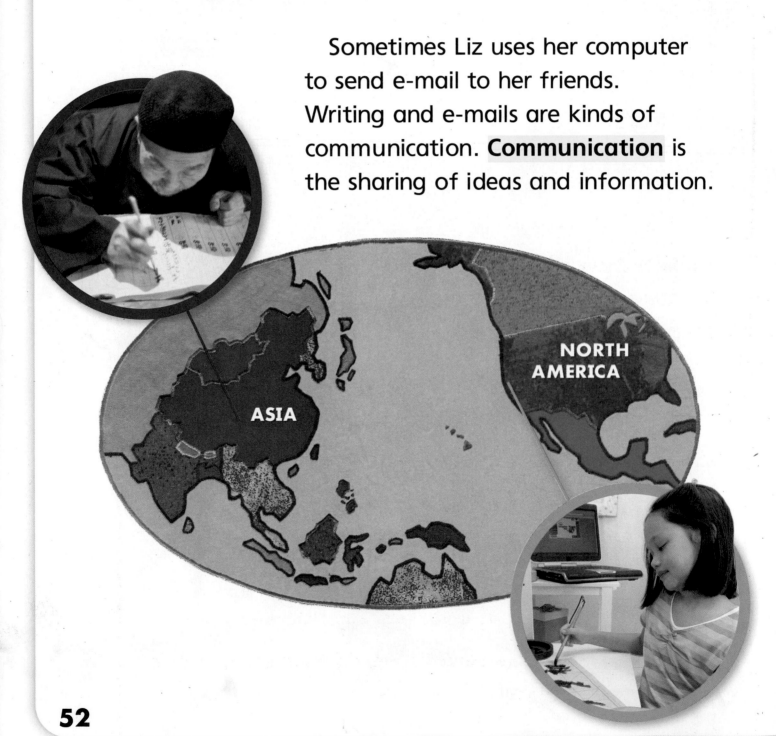

NORTH AMERICA

ASIA

A Closer Look

Communication

Today, communication is faster than ever. New ways of communication connect people all over the world. How have these tools made communication faster?

❶ satellite

❷ television

❸ telephone

❹ computer

Summary The lives of families have changed in many ways, but some things stay the same.

Review

❶ How is daily life now different from daily life in the past? How is it the same?

❷ **Vocabulary** How has **transportation** changed?

❸ **Activity** Make a chart to compare and contrast your family's life in the past and today.

❹ **Sequence** How was life different before people had electricity?

Points of View

The Sidewalk Reporter asks:
"How have changes made your life better?"

John

"I can call my friends on my cell phone."

Latisha

"I can do my homework on the computer."

View from the Past

Johannes Gutenberg: Communication

Long ago, books were written by hand, so there were not many of them. In about 1450, Johannes Gutenberg invented a way to print books faster. Then, more people could share ideas.

54

Carrie

"I can take an airplane to visit my grandmother."

Mr. Perez

"My grandson writes e-mails to me, but I also like it when he sends me a card in the mail."

Mrs. Patel

"I can buy frozen dinners at the store."

ANALYSIS SKILL

It's Your Turn

- Do any of these changes make a difference in your life? If so, which ones?
- What changes have made your life easier or better?

My Grandma's Stories

by Jorge Argueta

illustrated by Ana Ochoa

Mita's stories
filled her shack
with stars

Mita's stories
put smiles
on our faces

Mita's stories
are old
like the mountains

Los cuentos de Mita
hacen que su rancho
se llene de estrellas

Los cuentos de Mita
nos dibujan
sonrisas en el rostro

Los cuentos de Mita
son tan viejos
como las montañas

Mita's stories
are like the songs
of the crickets

If I close my eyes
I hear them
in the wind

Los cuentos de Mita
son como el canto
de los grillos

Si cierro los ojos
los escucho
en el viento

Response Corner

To what does the author
compare Mita's stories?

57

Avila Adobe

Get Ready

Don Francisco Avila built the Avila Adobe in 1818. It is the oldest house in Los Angeles. In 1971, an earthquake damaged the house. The home has been repaired. Today, the Avila Adobe is a museum. Visitors can see artifacts that show what family life was like in the 1840s.

Locate It

California

Los Angeles

What to See

clay oven

This couple is doing a traditional hat dance.

kitchen

bedroom

living room

A Virtual Tour

GO ONLINE

Visit VIRTUAL TOURS at
www.harcourtschool.com/hss

59

Review

💡 **Families** Today's families are different from those that lived long ago. Some things in families are still the same.

⭐ (Focus Skill) Sequence

Read the passage and finish the chart to show what you have learned about events in a family's history.

Lan Nguyen's ancestors came to California long ago. First, they traveled from Vietnam on a boat. Next, Lan's parents met and married. Last, they bought a house that Lan lives in today.

First	Next	Last
Lan's ancestors traveled from Vietnam.	_____ _____	_____ _____

Use Vocabulary

Write the word that completes each sentence.

① We live in a _____ of people in southern California.

② My _____ traveled here from Scotland long ago.

③ This old painting is an _____ from the past.

④ Events that happened in the past are part of _____.

⑤ Writing a letter is one kind of _____.

history
(p. 22)

community
(p. 24)

ancestors
(p. 36)

artifact
(p. 37)

communication
(p. 52)

Recall Facts

⑥ How have communities changed over time?

⑦ How can we show important events in order?

⑧ In what ways has transportation changed?

⑨ Which of these is a diagram that shows the parts of a family?

    A calendar   **C** time line

    B storyboard   **D** family tree

⑩ Which of these is a form of communication?

    A electricity   **C** cars

    B e-mail   **D** roads

Think Critically

⓫ **ANALYSIS SKILL** How can traditions from the past help us in the future?

⓬ **Make It Relevant** How does your heritage make your family special?

Apply Chart and Graph Skills

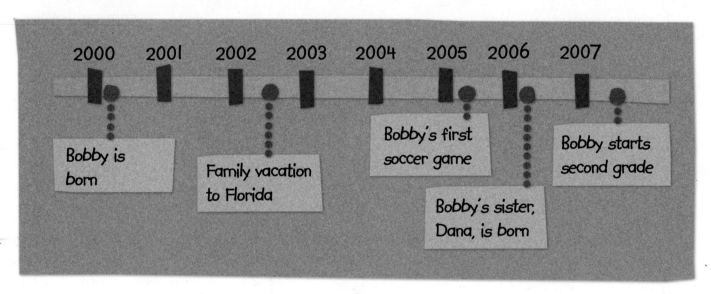

2000 2001 2002 2003 2004 2005 2006 2007

Bobby is born

Family vacation to Florida

Bobby's first soccer game

Bobby's sister, Dana, is born

Bobby starts second grade

⓭ In what year was Bobby born?

⓮ When was Bobby's first soccer game?

⓯ Was Dana born before or after the family vacation?

⓰ When did Bobby start second grade?

Apply Chart and Graph Skills

November

Sunday	Monday	Tuesday	Wednesday	Thursday	Friday	Saturday
				1	2	3
4	5	6 Election Day	7	8	9 Field Trip	10
11 Veterans Day	12	13	14	15	16	17
18	19	20	21	22 Thanksgiving	23	24
25	26	27	28	29	30	

⑰ On what day of the week does November begin?

⑱ What happens on November 9?

⑲ When is Veterans Day?

⑳ What holiday is on November 22?

Read More

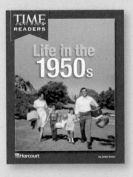

Family Memories by Jordan Brown

Life in the 1950s by Jordan Brown

Angel Island by Jordan Brown

Show What You Know

Unit Writing Activity

Go Back in Time Think about your community 100 years ago. How did people get around? What did they do for fun?

Write a Diary Entry Write a diary entry telling about a day in your life 100 years ago.

Unit Project

Storyboard Design a family history storyboard.

- Interview family members.
- Collect photographs or draw pictures of your family.
- Put the pictures in order.
- Share your storyboard.

GO ONLINE Visit ACTIVITIES at www.harcourtschool.com/hss

64

The Land Around Us

Start with the Standards

2.2 Students demonstrate map skills by describing the absolute and relative locations of people, places, and environments.

The Big Idea

The Land

Maps help us learn about the land and places around us. Different kinds of land and water can be found on a map.

What to Know

✔ How do maps help people locate places?

✔ What are some ways people use land in California?

✔ What are some landforms and countries on the continent of North America?

✔ Why do people move from one place to another?

Show What You Know

★ Unit 2 Test

✎ Writing: A Friendly Letter

✐ Unit Project: A Geography Bulletin Board

The Land Around Us

Talk About
The Land

" People visit California to see Yosemite National Park. "

"My compass keeps me from getting lost."

"The land looks the same now as it did to families who moved here long ago."

65

Vocabulary

location   The place where something is.

(page 76)

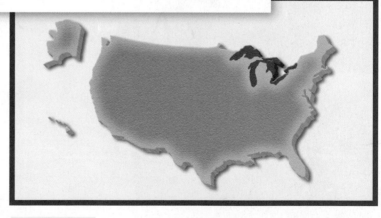

country   An area of land with its own people and laws.

(page 90)

landform   A kind of land with a special shape, such as a mountain, hill, or plain. (page 92)

cardinal directions The main directions of north, south, east, and west. (page 96)

immigrant   A person who comes from somewhere else to live in a country. (page 103)

GO ONLINE

INTERNET RESOURCES
Go to **www.harcourtschool.com/hss** to view Internet resources for this unit.

Reading Social Studies

(Focus Skill) # Compare and Contrast

As you read, be sure to compare and contrast. This will help you understand what you read.

● To compare, think about how people, places, or things are the same.

● To contrast, think about how people, places, or things are different.

Practice the Skill

Read the following paragraph.

Compare

Contrast

Santa Monica and South Lake Tahoe are two cities in California. Visitors to Santa Monica can swim or surf in the ocean. South Lake Tahoe is a good place to hike in the forests or ski and snowboard down the mountains. In both cities, people can fish. People can enjoy many activities in each place.

Santa Monica

South Lake Tahoe

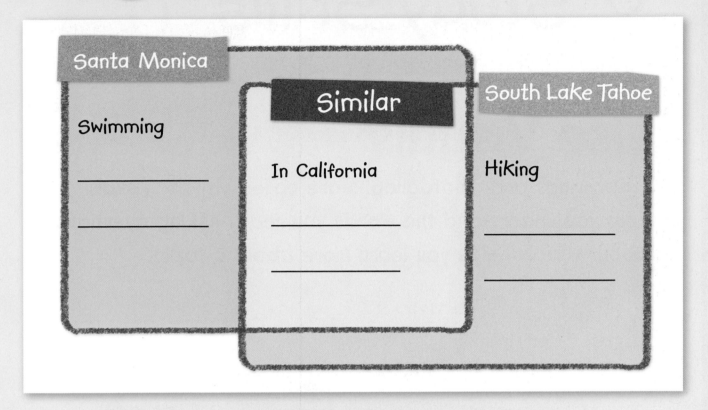

Santa Monica

Swimming

_____

_____

Similar

In California

_____

_____

South Lake Tahoe

Hiking

_____

_____

This chart shows how these two California cities are the same and how they are different. What can you add to the chart? Copy the chart and complete it.

Apply as You Read

As you read this unit, look for ways to compare and contrast places where people live.

Study Skills

Use Visuals

Drawings and photographs are called visuals. Visuals help you understand the words you read. Asking questions about visuals helps you learn more about a topic.

Practice the Skill

You can learn about the land around you by looking at visuals. Look at the photograph by Ansel Adams on the next page.

Answer these questions about the land in the photograph.

- Does this land look like the place where you live? How is it the same? How is it different?

- How do you think people use this land?

Apply as You Read

Preview the pages of this unit and look at the visuals. As you read, study the drawings and photographs to help you understand the land around you.

How the Prairie Became Ocean

by Joseph Bruchac

illustrated by David McCall Johnston

Storytelling is a part of many people's traditions.
Legends are a kind of story that teach a lesson
or help explain something. This is a legend of the
Yurok people.

Long ago, when there were no people, the ocean was a treeless plain. Thunder stood and looked over the land. He knew that soon people would be there.

"How will the people be able to live?" Thunder turned to his companion, Earthquake. "What do you think?" Thunder asked. "Should we place water here?"

Earthquake thought. "I believe we should do that," he said. "Far from here, at the end of the land, there is water. Salmon are swimming there."

So Earthquake and Water Panther went to the end of the land, where there was ocean. They picked up two big abalone shells and filled the shells with salt water. Then they carried the shells back to Thunder.

Earthquake began to walk around. As he walked, the ground sank beneath him. Water Panther filled the sunken ground with the salt water.

Now there was ocean where there had only been a treeless plain. Thunder rolled over the mountains and bent the trees down so they would grow on the land. Seals and salmon and whales swam through gullies made by the sinking land.

Beside the ocean, the land rose up into hills and animals came down from the mountains—deer, elk, foxes, and rabbits.

"Now this will be a good place for the people to live," Thunder said.

"This is a good place," Earthquake agreed. "Let us live here, too."

And so, to this day, Thunder and Earthquake live there, near the place they made the land into ocean for the people.

Response Corner

1 What does this legend explain?

2 **Make It Relevant** What description of California can you find in this legend?

Different Kinds of Maps

What to Know
How do maps help people locate places?

✓ There are many kinds of maps.

✓ Maps help people find locations.

Vocabulary
location
map title
map legend

Focus Skill
Compare and Contrast

California Standards
HSS 2.2, 2.2.2

There are many kinds of maps. Maps show **location**, or where places are. Some maps show small areas, such as parks. Others show large areas, such as cities, countries, or continents.

Maps have words and pictures to help you find places. This street map shows the locations of places on city streets. Read the **map title** to find out what a map is about. The title is usually at the top of a map. Read the **map legend** to find out what the map symbols stand for.

ANALYSIS SKILL On which street are the stores?

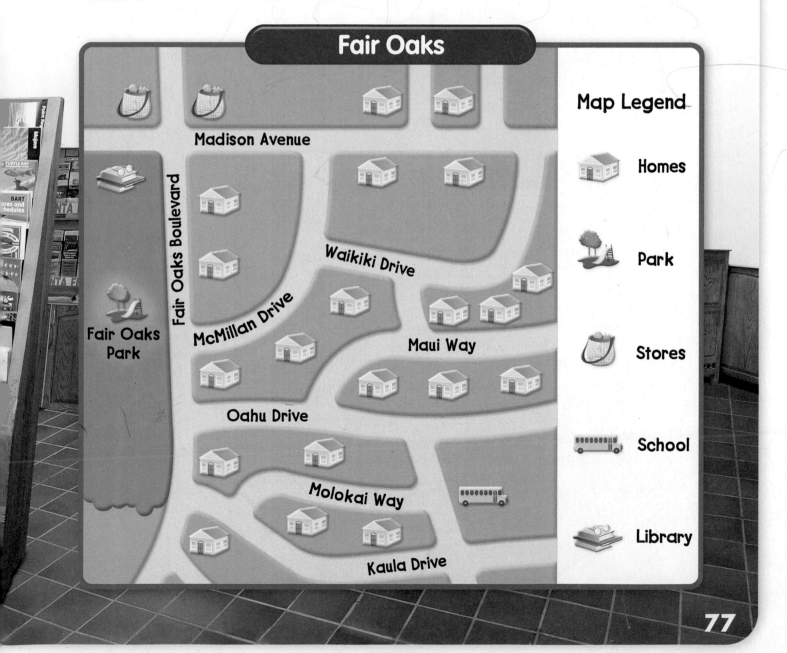

Fair Oaks

Madison Avenue

Fair Oaks Boulevard

Fair Oaks Park

Waikiki Drive

McMillan Drive

Maui Way

Oahu Drive

Molokai Way

Kaula Drive

Map Legend

Homes

Park

Stores

School

Library

A map can also help you find places that are indoors. This kind of map is called a floor plan. The floor plan on this page shows the location of rooms inside a school.

ANALYSIS SKILL What rooms are next to the art room?

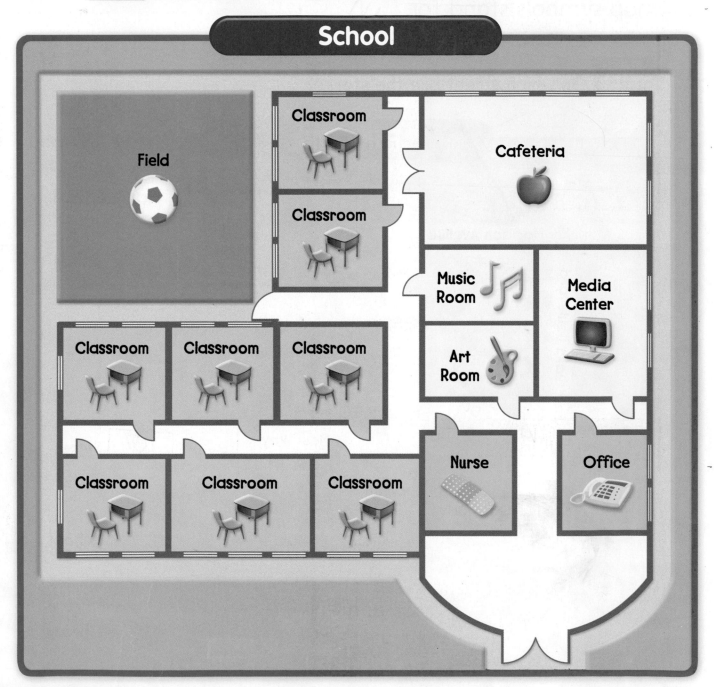

School

Field

Classroom

Classroom

Cafeteria

Classroom

Classroom

Classroom

Music Room

Media Center

Art Room

Classroom

Classroom

Classroom

Nurse

Office

Ranch Map

People have been making maps for a long time. This map is from about 1841. It shows the land around a ranch in Monterey County, California. Like maps of today, it shows places and things, such as mountains and rivers. There is even a picture of a bear that was often around the ranch. How could this map help a rancher?

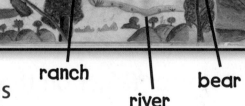

mountain

road

ranch

river

bear

Summary People use different kinds of maps to help them locate places.

Review

❶ How do maps help people find places?

❷ **Vocabulary** What does a **map legend** show?

❸ **Activity** Draw a map of your classroom. Make a map legend for your map.

❹ **Focus Skill** **Compare and Contrast** How are a floor plan and a street map alike? How are they different?

Read a Map Grid

◗ Why It Matters

One way to find locations on a map is to use a map grid. A **map grid** is a set of lines that divide a map into columns and rows of squares.

◗ What You Need to Know

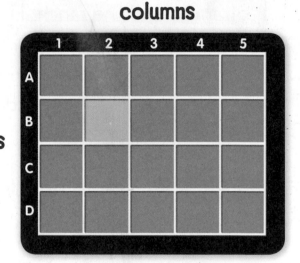

columns

rows

❶ Look at the grid. Put your finger on the gold square. Slide your finger left and right. This is row B.

❷ Put your finger on the gold square again. Slide your finger up and down. This is column 2.

❸ The gold square is at B-2 on the grid.

◗ Practice the Skill

This is a map grid of Red Bud.

❶ In which square is the school?

❷ What place is in B-5?

❸ In which square is the police station?

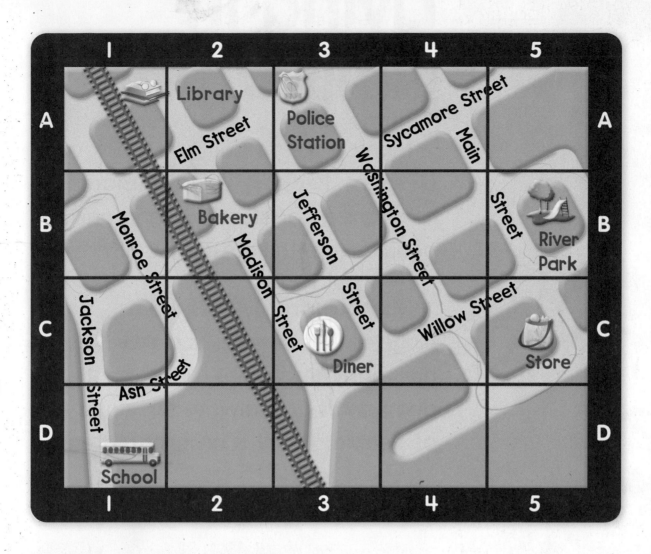

Apply What You Learned

Make It Relevant Make a map of your community. Add a map grid. Tell a classmate the row and column of the square in which a building is located. See if she or he can name that building.

Practice your map and globe skills with the **GeoSkills CD-ROM.**

Living in California

What to Know
What are some ways people use land in California?

✓ There are urban, suburban, and rural areas in California.

✓ Urban, suburban, and rural lands are different.

Vocabulary
state
city
urban
suburb
rural

Focus Skill
Compare and Contrast

California Standards
HSS 2.2.4

Many places in California look very different. People live in communities of all sizes. Together the land and people form the **state** of California.

Michael's family lives in Los Angeles. Los Angeles is a **city**. A city has many businesses, apartments, and homes. It is always busy and full of people. A city is an **urban** area.

Los Angeles

Elena's family lives in a suburban area in Agoura Hills. A **suburb** is a smaller community near a big city.

Suburbs are different from urban areas. They have quieter neighborhoods, fewer people, and less traffic. Homes in suburbs may have bigger yards. Some people live in a suburb and go into the city each day to work.

Agoura Hills

83

Kendra's family lives on a farm in a rural area in Yreka. **Rural** areas are in the country, far away from a city. Houses and buildings may be far apart. Kendra has to travel by car to visit her neighbors. A rural area is a quiet place.

Yreka farm

Hot, dry deserts, such as this one in Death Valley National Park, are also rural areas.

This map shows where people live in California. It shows urban and rural areas. It also shows the suburbs of some of the largest cities. Read the map legend to find out what the map symbols stand for.

ANALYSIS SKILL Where do most people live in California?

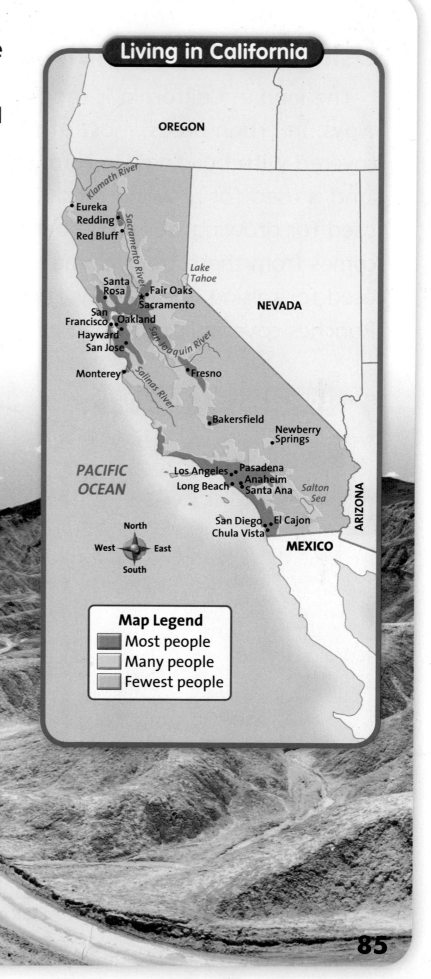

Living in California

OREGON

Klamath River

Eureka
Redding
Red Bluff

Sacramento River

Lake Tahoe

NEVADA

Santa Rosa
Fair Oaks
Sacramento

San Francisco
Oakland
Hayward
San Jose

San Joaquin River

Monterey
Salinas River
Fresno

Bakersfield

Newberry Springs

PACIFIC OCEAN

Los Angeles
Pasadena
Anaheim
Long Beach
Santa Ana

Salton Sea

ARIZONA

North
West   East
South

San Diego
Chula Vista
El Cajon

MEXICO

Map Legend
Most people
Many people
Fewest people

85

Using Land in California

The land in California is used in different ways. In urban areas, most of the land is covered with buildings. In rural areas, some land is used for growing food. Some land is used for growing trees. Lumber for houses comes from these trees. Some land is used for raising horses, cows, and sheep. Ranches cover miles of open land.

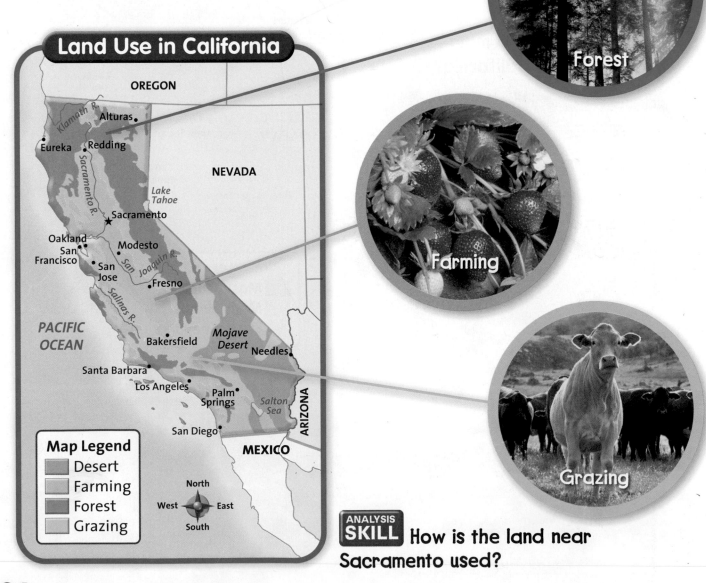

Forest

Farming

Grazing

Land Use in California

OREGON

NEVADA

Klamath R.

Alturas

Eureka Redding

Sacramento R.

Lake Tahoe

★ Sacramento

Oakland
San Francisco
Modesto

San Jose

San Joaquin R.

Fresno

Salinas R.

PACIFIC OCEAN

Bakersfield

Mojave Desert

Needles

Santa Barbara

Los Angeles

Palm Springs

Salton Sea

San Diego

ARIZONA

MEXICO

Map Legend

Desert
Farming
Forest
Grazing

North
West East
South

ANALYSIS SKILL How is the land near Sacramento used?

Cultural Heritage

Paul Bunyan Mountain and Blues Festival

Westwood was once one of the largest lumber towns in the West. Every year, the town celebrates its logging heritage with a festival. There is also a 24-foot-high statue of Paul Bunyan, the tall-tale logger, in downtown Westwood.

Summary The way land is used depends on whether it is in an urban area, a suburb, or a rural area.

Review

1. What are some ways people use land in California?

2. **Vocabulary** Why do some people like to live in a **suburb**?

3. **Write** Write three sentences describing the ways land is used in California.

4. **Compare and Contrast** How are urban and rural areas different?

Use a Map Scale

❱ Why It Matters

A map shows a place much smaller than it really is. A **map scale** is a part of a map that helps you find real distance. It helps you find out how far one place is from another place.

❱ What You Need to Know

Step 1 Lay a strip of paper between two places on a map.

Step 2 Mark the edge of the paper at each place.

Step 3 Place the paper along the map scale with one of the marks at zero. See how far it is to the second mark.

❱ Practice the Skill

❶ How many miles are there between Fresno and Barstow?

❷ How far is it from Redding to Sacramento?

❸ How far is it from Barstow to San Diego?

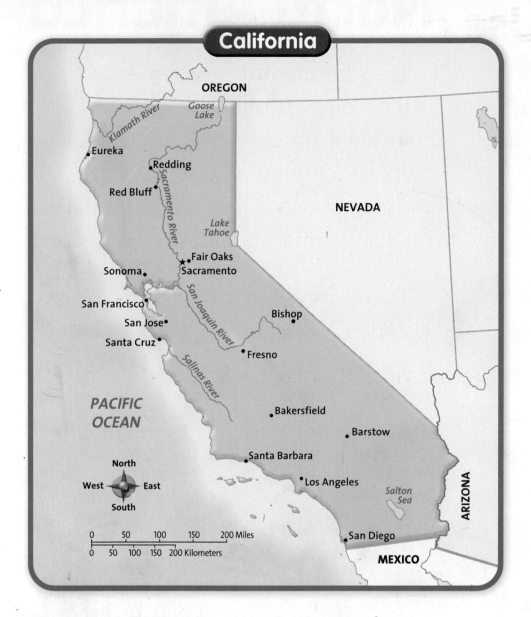

California

OREGON

Klamath River
Goose Lake

Eureka

Redding

Red Bluff

Sacramento River

Lake Tahoe

NEVADA

Fair Oaks
Sacramento

Sonoma

San Francisco

San Joaquin River

San Jose

Santa Cruz

Bishop

Salinas River

Fresno

PACIFIC OCEAN

Bakersfield

Barstow

North
West East
South

Santa Barbara

Los Angeles

Salton Sea

ARIZONA

0   50   100   150   200 Miles
0   50 100 150 200 Kilometers

San Diego

MEXICO

◗ Apply What You Learned

ANALYSIS SKILL **Make It Relevant** Find your community on a map. Use the map scale to measure the distance from your community to other places.

Practice your map and globe skills with the **GeoSkills CD-ROM.**

3

North America

The United States of America is the name of our country. A **country** is an area of land with its own people and its own laws. Our country is located on the continent of North America.

There are many countries in North America. Canada and Mexico, our neighbors, are big countries. Central America has many small countries that are also part of North America.

Sierra Nevada

What to Know
What are some landforms and countries on the continent of North America?

✓ There are many different landforms in North America.

✓ Countries, landforms, and bodies of water are shown on a map of North America.

Vocabulary
country
landform

Compare and Contrast

California Standards
HSS 2.2, 2.2.2

Fast Fact
The bald eagle is found only in North America, in places from Florida and Mexico to Alaska and Canada.

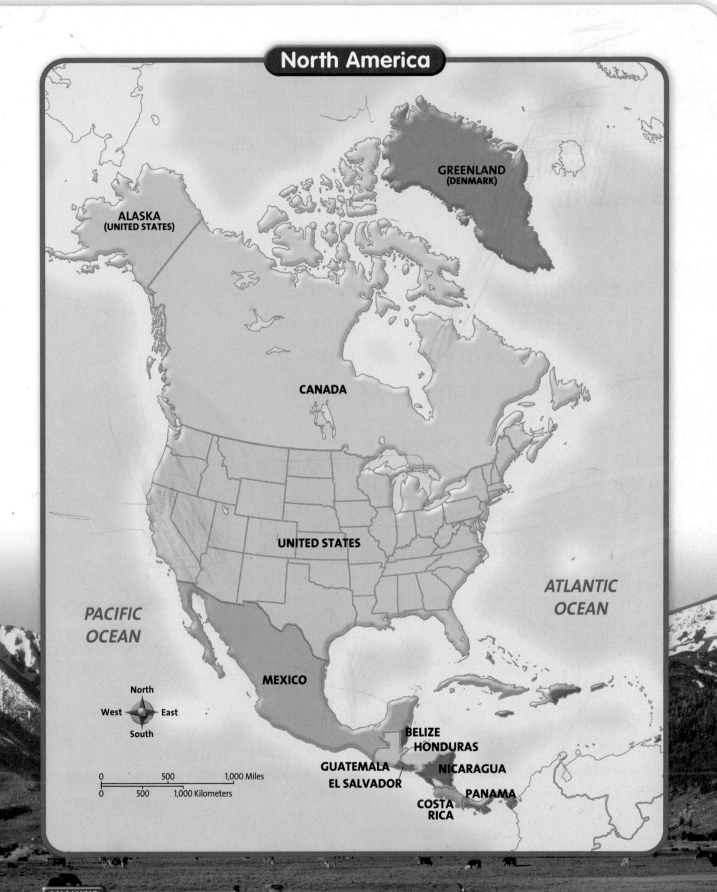

North America

GREENLAND
(DENMARK)

ALASKA
(UNITED STATES)

CANADA

UNITED STATES

PACIFIC
OCEAN

ATLANTIC
OCEAN

MEXICO

North
West — East
South

BELIZE
HONDURAS

GUATEMALA
EL SALVADOR

NICARAGUA

PANAMA

COSTA
RICA

0   500   1,000 Miles
0   500   1,000 Kilometers

ANALYSIS SKILL Why is Alaska, at the top left corner of Canada, shown in the same color as the United States?

Landforms

The land in North America is not the same everywhere. If an eagle flew across North America, it would see many different landforms. A **landform** is a kind of land with a special shape.

In the middle of our country, the eagle would look down on plains, or flat land. The Great Plains are in both the United States and Canada.

Onions are one of the many foods grown in California.

plains

92

hills

mountains

The eagle would also see land with many hills. A hill is land that rises above the land around it. A mountain is a very high hill. Mountains may have snow on their peaks even in the summer. A group of mountains is called a mountain range. Many mountain ranges stretch across parts of North America.

Bodies of Water

Besides land, the eagle would fly over many kinds of bodies of water. The biggest are oceans. North America lies between two oceans.

ANALYSIS SKILL Between which two oceans can you find North America?

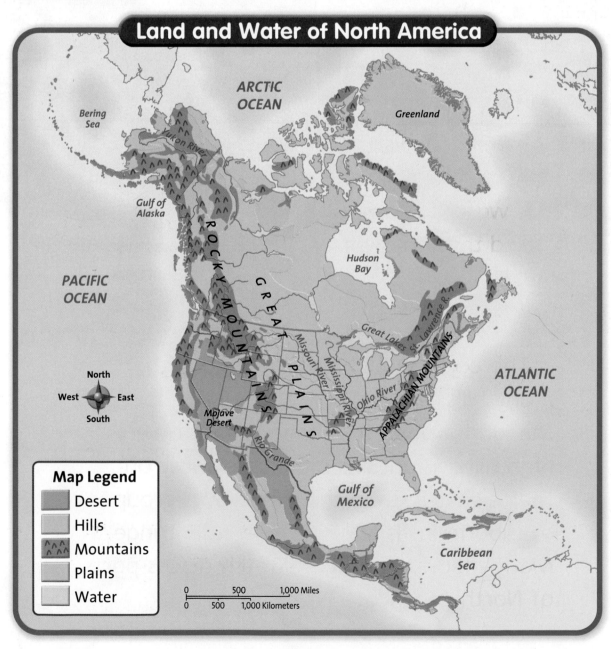

Land and Water of North America

ARCTIC OCEAN

Bering Sea

Greenland

Yukon River

Gulf of Alaska

ROCKY MOUNTAINS

Hudson Bay

PACIFIC OCEAN

GREAT PLAINS

Great Lakes

St. Lawrence R.

Missouri River

Mississippi River

Ohio River

APPALACHIAN MOUNTAINS

ATLANTIC OCEAN

North
West   East
South

Mojave Desert

Rio Grande

Gulf of Mexico

Caribbean Sea

Map Legend
- Desert
- Hills
- ^^ Mountains
- Plains
- Water

0   500   1,000 Miles
0   500   1,000 Kilometers

All over the land, there are rivers and lakes. A river is a stream of water that flows across the land. A lake is a body of water that has land all around it. The Great Lakes are large lakes located between the United States and Canada.

Summary A map of North America shows the countries, landforms, and bodies of water found on and around the continent.

The longest river in North America is the Mississippi River.

Review

1. 💡 What are some landforms and countries on the continent of North America?

2. **Vocabulary** What **landform** can you find in the middle of the United States?

3. ✏️ **Activity** Draw a map of North America. Label the countries, landforms, and bodies of water.

4. (Focus Skill) **Compare and Contrast** How are mountains different from hills?

95

Find Directions on a Map or Globe

North Pole

South Pole

❱ Why It Matters

Cardinal directions help you describe where places are on a map or globe. The **cardinal directions** are the main directions of north, south, east, and west.

The **equator** is an imaginary line that divides Earth in half. You can describe places on Earth as north or south of the equator.

North Pole

South Pole

❱ What You Need to Know

A **directional indicator** shows the cardinal directions on a map or globe.

❱ Practice the Skill

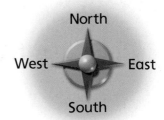

North

West   East

South

❶ What country is our neighbor to the north of the United States?

❷ What country is our neighbor to the south of the United States?

❸ In which direction would you travel to go from the Pacific Ocean to the Atlantic Ocean?

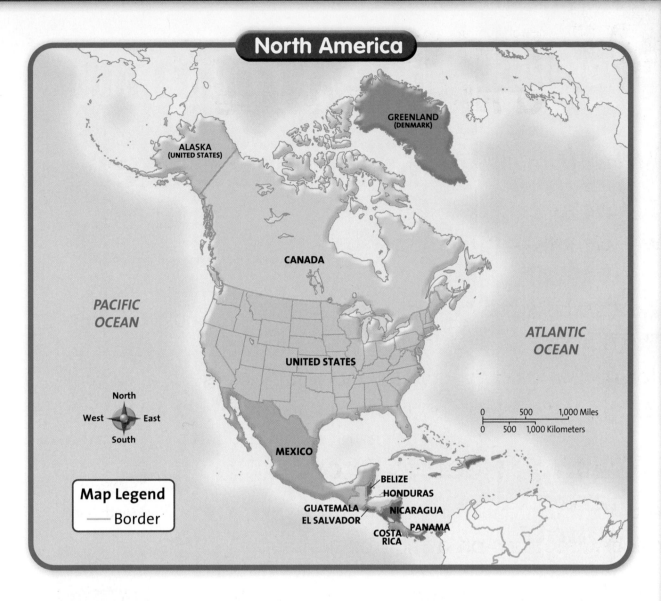

North America

GREENLAND
(DENMARK)

ALASKA
(UNITED STATES)

CANADA

PACIFIC
OCEAN

ATLANTIC
OCEAN

UNITED STATES

North

West — East

South

MEXICO

0   500   1,000 Miles
0   500   1,000 Kilometers

BELIZE
HONDURAS
GUATEMALA   NICARAGUA
EL SALVADOR
                    PANAMA
            COSTA
            RICA

Map Legend
— Border

◗ Apply What You Learned

ANALYSIS SKILL **Make It Relevant** With a classmate, identify some places in your classroom, school, or neighborhood. Use cardinal directions to describe how to get to them from where you are.

 Practice your map and globe skills with the **GeoSkills CD-ROM.**

Trustworthiness

Respect

Responsibility

Fairness

Caring

Patriotism

Why Character Counts

❓ How did Benjamin Banneker show patriotism?

Benjamin Banneker

When Benjamin Banneker was a young boy, he taught himself many things. Banneker read books to learn about math. He studied the sky at night to learn about the stars. He even copied the parts of his friend's watch and made a clock of his own. By the time Banneker was an adult, he was known for his work as a writer and as a scientist.

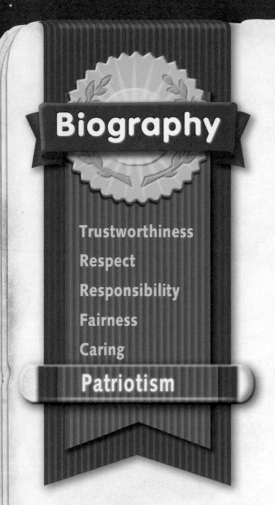

Benjamin Banneker helped measure the land for Washington, D.C.

The U.S. Postal Service issued a stamp in Banneker's honor.

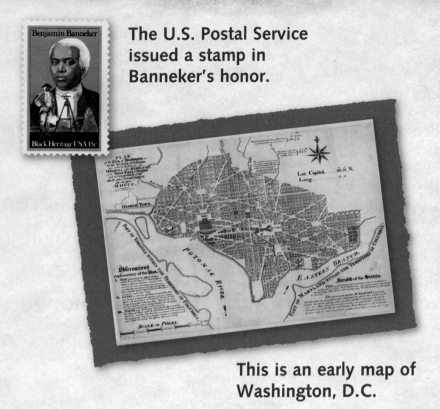

This is an early map of Washington, D.C.

Banneker wrote almanacs that gave weather information and other useful facts.

In 1791, Benjamin Banneker was asked to help survey, or measure, a piece of land. On this land, the new capital of the United States government would be built. Soon President George Washington hired Banneker as one of three surveyors to map out the new city. It was later named Washington, D.C. Banneker's work helped his country build a grand city for the new American government.

Bio Brief

1731   1806

Important Dates

1753 Teaches himself to build a clock

1791 Helps survey the land for the new capital, Washington, D.C.

1791 Publishes his first almanac

GO ONLINE
Interactive Multimedia Biographies
Visit MULTIMEDIA BIOGRAPHIES
at **www.harcourtschool.com/hss**

Moving from Place to Place

For thousands of years, American Indians were the only people living in North America. Then pioneers came from other places. A **pioneer** is someone who makes a home in a new area.

People come to the old Santa Barbara Mission to remember the past with celebrations like this art festival.

Some of the early pioneers in California were Spanish people from Mexico. They built missions along the west coast of the state. These were small communities built around churches. The missions had land that was good for ranches and farms. In time, towns grew up around the missions.

El Camino Real

El Camino Real was a road that stretched more than 600 miles from San Diego to Sonoma. Its name means "the Royal Road." Along the road were 21 missions. A person could walk from each mission to the next in just one day.

El Camino Real

Legend

— El Camino Real 1823

🏠 Mission

Across the United States, near the Atlantic Ocean, many more people were making new homes. Soon, some of them began to move west. They were looking for good land to farm. They traveled over plains on foot, on horseback, and in wagons. Later, trains moved people over and around mountains. Before long, there were farms, ranches, towns, and cities all across the country.

Strawberry Valley, 1866

"Go West, young man,

Some people came from far across the oceans. These people were **immigrants**, or people who come from somewhere else to live in a country. They made the journey for different reasons. Some came to look for jobs or land. Others wanted freedom or adventure. People still come to the United States for all of these reasons.

Angel Island, 1925

San Francisco International Airport, 2004

and grow up with the country."

John B.L. Soule, Editorial in the Terre Haute Express, 1851

Life in a New Country

Starting over in a new country is not easy. Immigrants have to find new jobs and homes. Often they have to learn a new language and new customs, or ways of doing things.

In this community in San Francisco, people keep up their Chinese language, customs, and traditions.

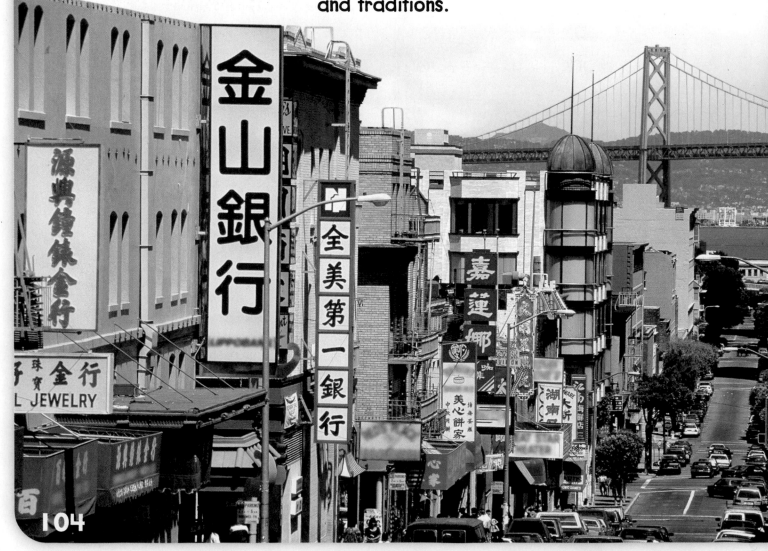

Many people in California are recent immigrants. They come from countries such as Mexico, El Salvador, Vietnam, and India. Some come to find work. Others come for a safer place to live. They keep some of their heritage while learning new American ways.

This Sikh community shares their food traditions at a festival.

Summary People move from one place to another to find work, land, freedom, and safety.

Review

1. Why do people move from one place to another?

2. **Vocabulary** From where do **immigrants** come?

3. **Activity** Interview a family member. Find out when, how, and why your family moved to your community.

4. **Focus Skill** **Compare and Contrast** How are a pioneer and an immigrant alike?

Follow a Route

❱ Why It Matters

A map can show you where places are and how to get to them.

❱ What You Need to Know

The path you follow from one place to another is called a **route**. Highways are routes between towns and cities. Each highway has a number. A directional indicator tells you in which direction you are going when you follow a route.

❱ Practice the Skill

❶ Which highway goes from Sacramento to San Diego?

❷ In which direction would you travel on Highway 101 to go from San Francisco to Los Angeles?

❸ Which highways connect California to Nevada?

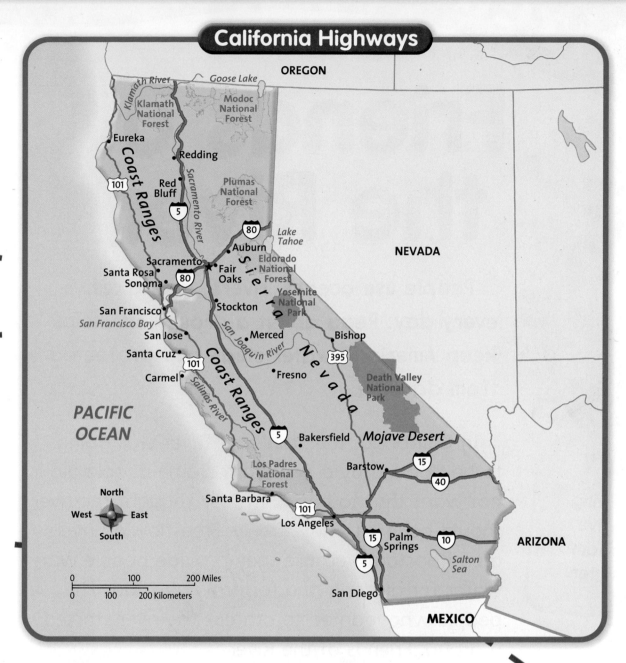

California Highways

OREGON

Goose Lake

Klamath River

Klamath National Forest

Modoc National Forest

Eureka

Redding

Coast Ranges

101

Red Bluff

Sacramento River

5

Plumas National Forest

80

Lake Tahoe

NEVADA

Auburn

Sacramento

Santa Rosa

Sonoma

80

Fair Oaks

Eldorado National Forest

Sierra Nevada

Yosemite National Park

San Francisco

Stockton

San Francisco Bay

San Joaquin River

Merced

Bishop

San Jose

395

Santa Cruz

101

Fresno

Carmel

PACIFIC OCEAN

Salinas River

Coast Ranges

Death Valley National Park

5

Bakersfield

Mojave Desert

Los Padres National Forest

Barstow

15

North

West   East

South

Santa Barbara

40

101

Los Angeles

15

Palm Springs

10

ARIZONA

5

Salton Sea

0   100   200 Miles

0   100   200 Kilometers

San Diego

MEXICO

◗ Apply What You Learned

ANALYSIS SKILL **Make It Relevant** Draw a map to show your route to school. Add a directional indicator to show directions.

 Practice your map and globe skills with the **GeoSkills CD-ROM.**

Friends of the River

People use oceans, rivers, and lakes every day. Read about a group that helps keep America's water clean and protected from damage.

In California, the Stanislaus River was going to be flooded by a new dam. Some people did not want that to happen. They thought the river should be left to flow freely. Free-flowing rivers are important because they provide people with water for drinking and for growing food. The people who wanted to protect the river started a group, Friends of the River.

Free-flowing rivers give Californians clean water.

Rivers are places where people can fish, raft, and kayak.

Today, Friends of the River has almost 6,000 members. They tell others about problems that California's rivers and streams may have. They work together to protect those bodies of water for the future.

Members of Friends of the River teach others important things about water.

Did You Know?

Did you know that there are ways in which you can conserve water where you live? You can save water if you:

★ Shorten your shower by a few minutes.

★ Turn off the water while you brush your teeth.

Think About It!

Make It Relevant Why should you care about our nation's bodies of water?

COVERED WAGONS, BUMPY TRAILS

by Verla Kay

illustrated by S. D. Schindler

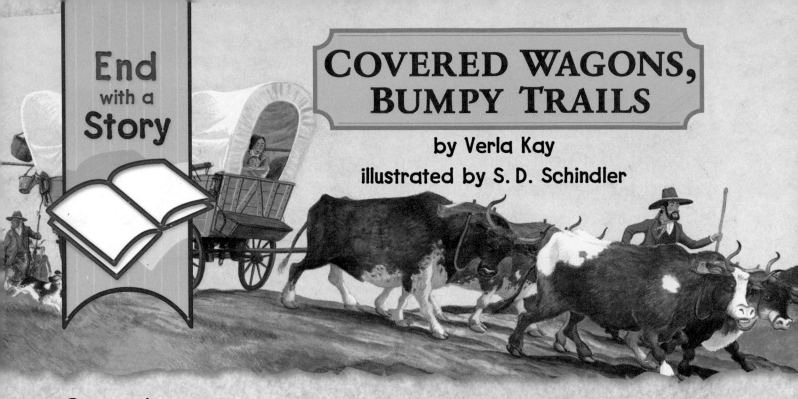

Covered wagon,
Bumpy road.
Plodding oxen,
Heavy load.

Mother, Father,
Baby John,
Bouncing, jouncing,
Moving on.

Fodder, water,
Guns and tools,
Clothes and blankets,
Stubborn mules.

Falter, flounder,
WHOOPS! In ditch.
Wiggle, wriggle,
Try a switch.

THUNDER! LIGHTNING!
Floods of rain.
Mucky, muddy,
Wet terrain.

Mother, Father,
Baby John,
Pushing forward,
Struggle on.

Weary, bleary,
Sweaty, hot.
End of day,
A camping spot.

Dry chips burning,
Steaks of snakes.
Coffee brewing,
Johnnycakes.

Rocky Mountains,
Massive, steep.
Rugged trail,
Wagons creep.

Dumping, tossing,
Trinkets, trunk.
Cookstove, treasures—
Now they're junk.

Hot sun swelters,
Parched land, dry.
Thick dust swirls,
Choking sky.

Mother, Father,
Baby John,
Plodding forward,
Struggle on.

Pushing, shoving,
Top of crest.
Fire, blankets,
Well-earned rest.

Frosty, frigid,
Icy air.
Lacy snowflakes
Everywhere.

Plunging, slipping,
Stuck in snow.
Frozen wheels,
"Oxen, WHOA!"

Mother, Father,
Baby John,
Walking slowly,
Trudging on.

Moving forward,
End of trail.
Meadows, poppies,
Soft brown quail.

Building cabins,
Clearing lands.
Rustic timbers,
Helping hands.

Mother, Father,
Baby John,
Fleecy flannel
Nightclothes on.

Sturdy windows,
Heavy doors.
Warm and safe now,
Happy snores.

Response Corner

How is this family's move
to a new place the same
as a family's move today?
How is it different?

Joshua Tree National Park

Get Ready

Joshua Tree National Park is located where the Mojave Desert and the Colorado Desert meet. Many people think of a desert as a place with little life. But visitors to the park will see many kinds of plants growing and a variety of animals who make the park their home.

Locate It

California

Joshua Tree National Park

What to See

Joshua trees grow only in a few places in North America. At the park, most of the trees are found growing in the Mojave Desert, which has a slightly cooler and wetter climate than the Colorado Desert has.

cactus wren

desert tortoise

hedgehog cactus

People and animals can find water and shade at one of the park's five desert palm oases.

A Virtual Tour

GO ONLINE

Visit VIRTUAL TOURS at www.harcourtschool.com/hss

Review

💡 **The Land** Maps help us learn about the land and places around us. Different kinds of land and water can be found on a map.

(Focus Skill) Compare and Contrast

Copy and fill in the Compare and Contrast chart to show how urban and suburban areas are alike and different.

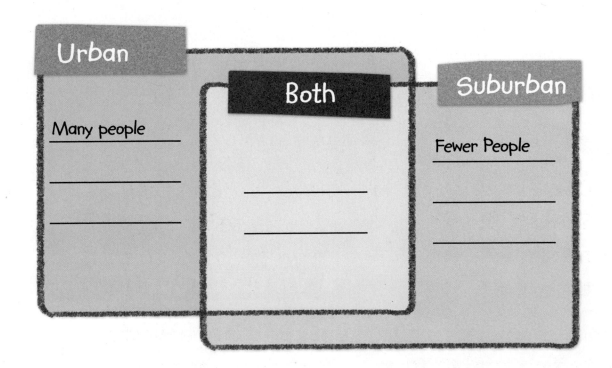

Urban

Many people

_____

_____

Both

_____

_____

Suburban

Fewer People

_____

_____

Use Vocabulary

Match the word to its meaning.

1 A kind of land with a special shape.

2 A person who comes from somewhere else to live in a country.

3 An area of land with its own people and laws.

4 The place where something is.

5 The main directions of north, south, east, and west.

location
(p. 76)

country
(p. 90)

landform
(p. 92)

cardinal directions
(p. 96)

immigrant
(p. 103)

Recall Facts

6 What does a map's title tell you?

7 How is rural land used in California?

8 What is a group of mountains called?

9 Who were the first people to live in California?

A Spanish people   **C** American Indians

B people from the   **D** people from China
    east coast

10 Why did people from the east coast move west?

A to find land to farm   **C** to find freedom

B to ride on trains   **D** to learn new
                                 customs

Think Critically

11. **ANALYSIS SKILL** In what ways might immigrants keep their own heritage in a new country?

12. **Make It Relevant** How might your family trips be different if you had no maps?

Apply Map and Globe Skills

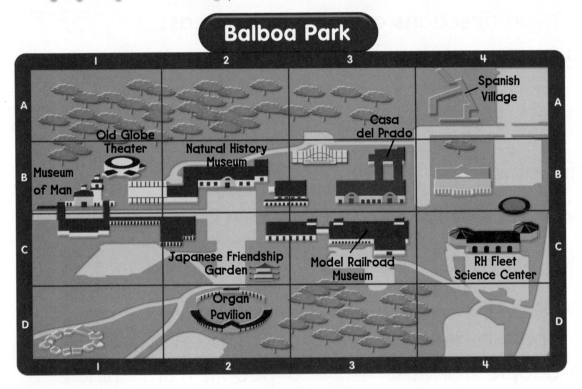

Balboa Park

13. In which square is the Spanish Village?

14. What place is in D-2?

15. What place is in B-3?

16. What two places are in B-1?

Apply Map and Globe Skills

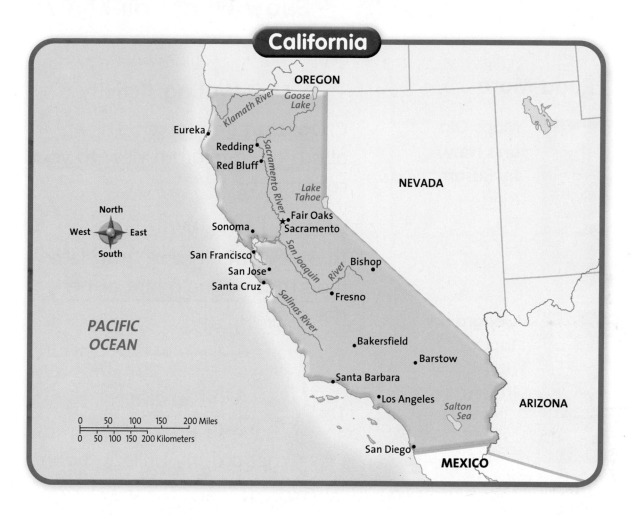

California

OREGON

Klamath River

Goose Lake

Eureka

Redding

Red Bluff

Sacramento River

Lake Tahoe

NEVADA

North

West   East

South

Sonoma

Fair Oaks

Sacramento

San Francisco

San Jose

Santa Cruz

San Joaquin River

Bishop

Fresno

Salinas River

PACIFIC OCEAN

Bakersfield

Barstow

Santa Barbara

Los Angeles

Salton Sea

ARIZONA

| 0 | 50 | 100 | 150 | 200 Miles |

| 0 | 50 | 100 | 150 | 200 Kilometers |

San Diego

MEXICO

⑰ Which California city is west of Sacramento?

⑱ What city is south of Los Angeles?

⑲ What state is north of California?

⑳ In which direction would you go if you traveled from Redding, California, to Nevada?

Read More

Maps Old and New by Susan Ring

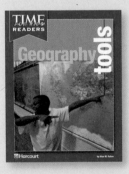

Geography Tools by Alan M. Ruben

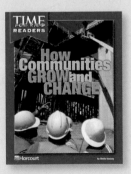

How Communities Grow and Change by Sheila Sweeny

Show What You Know

Unit Writing Activity

Choose an Immigrant Think about an immigrant new to your community.

Write a Letter Write a letter to a new immigrant. Include a map that will help him or her get around.

Unit Project

Bulletin Board Design a geography bulletin board.

- Think of ideas for the design.
- Gather materials.
- Decorate and label each section.
- Invite other classes to see the bulletin board.

GO ONLINE Visit ACTIVITIES at www.harcourtschool.com/hss

Governing the People

Start with the Standards

2.3 Students explain governmental institutions and practices in the United States and other countries.

The Big Idea

Government

A government makes laws to maintain order and help people get along.

What to Know

✓ How are the people in our country alike and different?

✓ How do community and state governments make and carry out laws?

✓ Who makes the laws for the United States?

✓ How do other nations make their laws?

✓ What are some things nations do to get along with one another?

Show What You Know

★ Unit 3 Test

✎ Writing: A Letter

✐ Unit Project: A Lawmaker Role Play

Governing the People

" The Supreme Court makes sure laws are fair. "

"American citizens are proud of their country."

"People visit Washington, D.C., to see many government buildings."

Vocabulary

citizen A person who lives in and belongs to a community.
(page 132)

government A group of citizens that runs a community, state, or country. (page 136)

law A rule that citizens must follow. (page 136)

President The leader of the United States government. (page 147)

vote A choice that gets counted. (page 150)

GO
ONLINE

INTERNET RESOURCES
Go to **www.harcourtschool.com/hss** to view Internet resources for this unit.

Reading Social Studies

⭐ Focus Skill Main Idea and Details

When you read for information, look for the main ideas and important details.

● The main idea is the most important part of what you are reading. In most paragraphs, the first sentence tells the main idea.

● The details explain the main idea. They most often follow the main idea sentence.

Practice the Skill

Read the following paragraph.

Main Idea   Our town is planning a new community center.

Detail   The center will be big enough for special events. It will have classes and fun activities for adults. It will also have after-school programs for children. Our new community center will have something for everyone!

Apply What You Learned

Main Idea

Our town is planning a new community center.

Details

It will be big enough for special events.	____________ ____________	____________ ____________

This chart shows the main idea and one detail from what you just read. What other details can you add to the chart? Copy the chart and complete it.

Apply as You Read

As you read this unit, look for the main idea and details about what governments do.

Study Skills

Build Vocabulary

You can use a word web to learn new words and connect ideas. In the center is a word or an idea. Around it are other words that link to the center.

Practice the Skill

Think about everything you know about a community. Copy Tina's word web shown on the next page.

● Add more words about communities.

● What do the words tell you about a community?

126

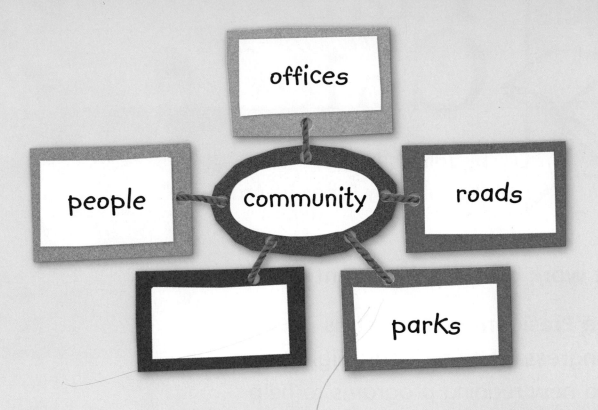

offices

people

community

roads

parks

Welcome to California

Apply as You Read

Make a word web for <u>government</u>. As you read this unit, add vocabulary words, important ideas, and other information to the web to show how they are connected.

Hail to the Chief

by John P. Riley
illustrated by Ruben De Anda

What work does the President do?

The President recommends new laws to Congress. The President might want to add new reading programs to help schoolchildren, or make it easier for sick people to buy medicine. For the President's ideas to become law, Congress must pass the law (agree to it) and provide the money to make it work.

The President enforces the law. The President is the top law officer in the nation, with the power to make sure citizens obey the laws of our country. In rare — but dramatic — times, the President can also order army troops to enforce laws.

The President is host to other nation's leaders. The President invites other world leaders to his home, the White House, to have meetings and to show off American hospitality. When the President and first lady host a dinner party for important visitors, the dinner menu usually includes favorite foods from the guest's country.

The President is a symbol of American leadership. He is the one person who represents our nation at home and around the world. Being President of the United States is a difficult job, with many tough choices to make. Great power comes with great responsibility.

Response Corner

Make It Relevant Would you like to be President? Why or why not?

What to Know
How are the people in our country alike and different?

✔ Many kinds of people live in the United States.

✔ Every citizen has rights and responsibilities.

Vocabulary
culture
citizen
right
freedom
responsibility

Focus Skill
Main Idea and Details

California Standards
HSS 2.3

A Country of Many People

A mosaic is a picture made up of tiles of many colors. Our country is like a mosaic. It is made up of people who speak many languages and do many jobs.

People come to our country from all over the world. They bring with them their own cultures. A **culture** is the way a group of people lives. What they eat, how they dress, and what they believe are parts of their culture.

We are different in many ways, but we are all citizens. A **citizen** is a person who belongs to a community.

What does it mean to be a citizen? In the United States, it means having the same **rights**, or freedoms, as others. **Freedom** is the right of people to make their own choices.

Americans have certain freedoms. We can live and work where we want. We can follow our religious beliefs and share our ideas.

Freedom of speech

Freedom of the press

Freedom of religion

Along with our freedoms, we have responsibilities. A **responsibility** is something a citizen should take care of or do. Citizens are responsible for taking care of themselves and others.

Making the <u>Arms Wide Open</u> mural

Arms Wide Open

The students at Vina Danks Middle School made a mural about their community. They wanted to include the different people who live there. At the center is Cesar Chavez. He thought people should show responsibility by helping make their communities better.

Summary In our country, people of all cultures have the same rights and responsibilities.

Review

1. How are the people in our country alike and different?

2. **Vocabulary** Name a **responsibility** a citizen of a community has.

3. **Activity** Make a collage that shows different people in our country and their customs.

4. **Main Idea and Details** What does it mean to be a citizen of the United States?

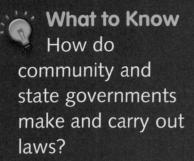

What to Know
How do community and state governments make and carry out laws?

City and state governments make laws to keep citizens safe.

Vocabulary
government
law
consequence
mayor
council
judge
governor
legislature

 **Main Idea and Details**

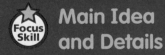 California Standards
HSS 2.3.1

Community and State Governments

Each community has a government. A **government** is a group of citizens that runs a community. It protects all people and their rights. The government passes laws to help people get along and stay safe. A **law** is a rule that citizens must follow. The government also makes sure the laws are followed.

Some citizens do not obey the laws. People who break laws must face the consequences. A **consequence** is something that happens because of what a person does. Lawbreakers may have to do work for the community or pay money to the government. People who break the most important laws must go to jail.

Street signs show laws everyone must follow.

Most community governments have three parts. A **mayor** is a citizen who leads a town or city. The mayor makes sure that the community is a good place to live.

The **council** is a group of people chosen by the citizens to make choices for them. In many communities, the council and the mayor make laws.

Government Leaders

Mayor

2004 RALLY FOR KIDS

Mayor Gavin Newsom of San Francisco

Courts are another part of community government. A court decides if someone has broken a law and what the consequences should be. A **judge** is a person in charge of a court. Judges make sure that the courts carry out laws fairly.

Who are the government leaders where you live?

City Council

Cynthia Sterling of Fresno city council

Judge

Judge Kirk H. Nakamura of Orange County

KIRK H. NAKAMURA
JUDGE

Like a community government, a state government has three parts. A **governor** leads the state. He or she makes sure that laws are carried out. The governor also suggests new laws.

The state legislature is like a community council, but it is much larger. Members of the **legislature** are the lawmakers for the state. They are chosen by the citizens of all the state's communities.

The state also has courts. Judges decide if someone has broken state laws. Many times, judges also decide the consequences for breaking the law.

Governor Arnold Schwarzenegger

Community and state governments do different jobs. Community governments work for the people of their community. They run the police and fire departments and plan buildings and parks.

State governments work for all of the people in a state. They take care of state roads and highways. In an emergency, the state government helps people get the food and shelter they need.

Summary Community and state governments make and carry out laws and take care of their citizens.

Review

1 How do community and state governments make and carry out laws?

2 Vocabulary What is the job of the **legislature**?

3 Write Write a letter to your community council about a law you think your community needs.

4 Main Idea and Details Why would a lawbreaker have to pay money to the government?

Find States and Capitals

> ## Why It Matters

Our country has 50 states. California is one of the largest states.

United States

ARCTIC OCEAN

RUSSIA

ALASKA

CANADA

Juneau ★

PACIFIC OCEAN

CANADA

Olympia ★
WASHINGTON

★ Salem

OREGON

Helena ★
MONTANA

★ Boise
IDAHO

NORTH DAKOTA
★ Bismarck

SOUTH DAKOTA
★ Pierre

MINNESOTA

St. Paul ★

Lake Superior

MICHIGAN

Lake Huron

WISCONSIN
Madison ★

Lansing ★
Lake Michigan
Lake Erie

WYOMING

Cheyenne ★

NEVADA
Carson City ★

Sacramento ★

Salt Lake City ★

UTAH

NEBRASKA

Lincoln ★

IOWA Des Moines ★

OHIO
Columbus ★
INDIANA

ILLINOIS
Springfield ★ Indianapolis ★

Denver ★
COLORADO

Topeka ★
KANSAS

MISSOURI
Jefferson City ★

Charleston
Frankfort ★
KENTUCKY

CALIFORNIA

PACIFIC OCEAN

ARIZONA

Santa Fe ★

NEW MEXICO

★ Phoenix

OKLAHOMA
Oklahoma City ★

ARKANSAS
Little Rock ★

Nashville ★
TENNESSEE

Atlanta ★
ALABAMA

MISSISSIPPI

Jackson ★ Montgomery ★

TEXAS

LOUISIANA
Baton Rouge ★

Austin ★

Tallahassee

Honolulu ★

HAWAII

PACIFIC OCEAN

MEXICO

Gulf of Mexico

What You Need to Know

You can find cities and states on a map. A **capital** is a city in which the government of a state or country meets. A **border** is a line that shows where a state or a country ends.

NEW HAMPSHIRE
VERMONT   MAINE
          ★ Augusta
NEW YORK   ★ Montpelier
Lake   ★ Concord
Ontario   ★ Boston
Albany ★   MASSACHUSETTS
Hartford ★ RHODE ISLAND ★
              Providence
PENNSYLVANIA CONNECTICUT
Harrisburg ★ Trenton
Annapolis   NEW JERSEY
      ★ ★ Dover DELAWARE
      ⊛ Washington, D.C.
          MARYLAND
      WEST VIRGINIA
Richmond   VIRGINIA
★ Raleigh
NORTH CAROLINA
★ Columbia
SOUTH CAROLINA
          ATLANTIC
GEORGIA   OCEAN

FLORIDA

North
West — East
South

Map Legend
⊛ National capital
★ State capital
— Border

Practice the Skill

① Find California on the map. What is the capital city?

② What states are found along the border of California?

Apply What You Learned

ANALYSIS SKILL List the capital cities of the states that are found along the border of California.

Practice your map and globe skills with the **GeoSkills CD-ROM.**

Our National Government

What to Know
Who makes the laws for the United States?

✓ Our country's government has three branches that follow the Constitution.

Vocabulary
Congress
tax
President
election
Supreme Court
Constitution

Main Idea and Details

California Standards
HSS 2.3, 2.3.1

Our country's government has three parts, or branches, just as community and state governments do. The legislative branch makes the laws. The executive branch carries out the laws. The judicial branch makes sure that the laws are fair.

White House

Washington, D.C.

The capital of our country is Washington, D.C. The White House, the Capitol building, and the Supreme Court are located there. Memorials and monuments on the National Mall honor past Presidents and war heroes.

Washington Monument

Supreme Court

Capitol

Congress, the legislative branch, makes the laws. The members of Congress are chosen by citizens of all 50 states. Besides making laws, they also decide on the taxes people will pay. A **tax** is money paid to the government. It pays for things that citizens need, such as schools, police protection, and libraries.

The National Guard helps during emergencies.

Many members of the armed forces serve in other countries.

In the United States, citizens choose a **President**. The President's job is to carry out laws and make sure that the country is a good place to live.

An **election** is an event in which citizens choose leaders. The citizens of our country decide who will be President and who will be in Congress.

"We will always remember. We will always be proud. We will always be prepared, so we may always be free."

President Ronald Reagan

Ronald Reagan, *The Greatest Speeches of Ronald Reagan,* NewsMax.com, Inc., 2001.

President Bush promises to work for the people.

The **Supreme Court** decides on laws for the entire country. It has nine judges. Each must be chosen by the President and agreed to by Congress. These judges make sure that the laws match what is in the Constitution.

The Supreme Court

The **Constitution** is the written set of rules that the government must follow. It explains how our government is to work.

ANALYSIS SKILL Why is the Constitution an important document?

The Constitution

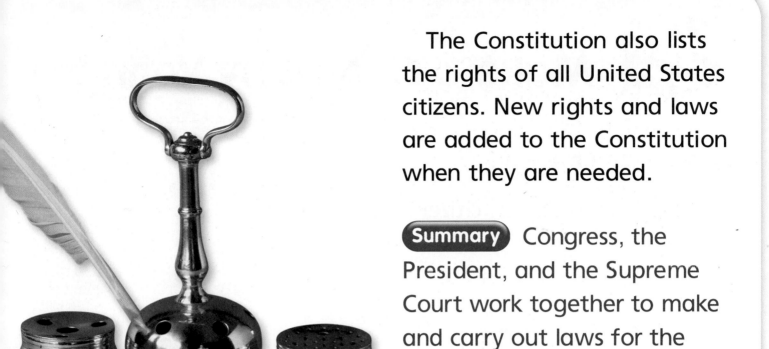

The Constitution also lists the rights of all United States citizens. New rights and laws are added to the Constitution when they are needed.

Summary Congress, the President, and the Supreme Court work together to make and carry out laws for the United States.

Review

1. 💡 Who makes the laws for the United States?

2. **Vocabulary** What does the **Constitution** explain?

3. ✏️ **Activity** Make a chart to show what each of the three branches of government does.

4. ⭐ **Main Idea and Details** What are the three branches of government?

Make a Choice by Voting

❯ Why It Matters

In the United States, citizens choose their leaders. They vote in an election. A **vote** is a choice that gets counted.

❯ What You Need to Know

❶ Before people vote, they think about who will do the best job.

❷ To vote in most elections, people mark a ballot. A **ballot** lists all of the choices. Voters mark their choice in secret. The ballots are not counted until everyone has voted.

❸ The winner of an election is the person who gets the most votes. This is called **majority rule**. Majority means "more than half."

Vote for one

Vivian _____
Eric _____
Jennifer _____
Tony ✓_____

VOTE

▶ Practice the Skill

Before   Imagine that your classroom is a community that wants to choose a new mayor. Four people want to lead the community. Only one of them can be mayor.

During   Make ballots that list the name of each person who wants to be mayor. Give each citizen a ballot to mark.

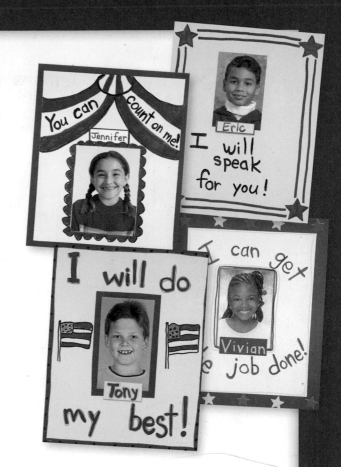

After   When everyone has voted, collect the ballots. Count the votes. The winner is the person who gets the most votes.

Vivian	Eric	Jennifer	Tony
ⅢⅢⅢ	ⅢⅢⅢⅢⅢ	Ⅲ	ⅢⅢ

▶ Apply What You Learned

Make It Relevant   Use voting as a way to make other choices in your classroom.

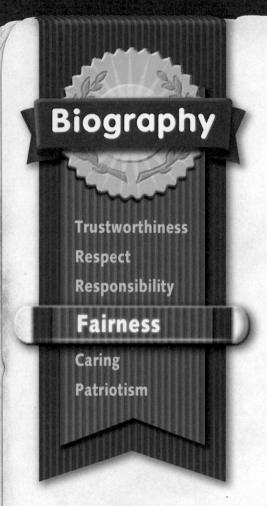

Trustworthiness
Respect
Responsibility
Fairness
Caring
Patriotism

Thurgood Marshall

Thurgood Marshall helped change the laws of the United States. When Marshall was a young boy, his father taught him to speak up for what he believed in. Thurgood Marshall went on to use this skill when he became a lawyer. He spent his life fighting for equal rights.

Why Character Counts

❔ **Why do you think Thurgood Marshall worked for laws to treat people fairly?**

Thurgood Marshall was the first African American Supreme Court Justice.

Thurgood Marshall said that schoolchildren cannot be separated because of their races.

When he retired, Justice Marshall had served longer than all but one of the justices of the Supreme Court.

In 1967, Thurgood Marshall was selected to be a justice, or judge, of the Supreme Court of the United States. Congress had to approve. President Lyndon Johnson told Congress this about Marshall: "It is the right thing to do, the right time to do it, the right man and the right place."* Thurgood Marshall was a respected justice of the Supreme Court for 24 years.

*President Lyndon Johnson. www.oyez.org

Interactive Multimedia Biographies
Visit MULTIMEDIA BIOGRAPHIES
at www.harcourtschool.com/hss

Bio Brief

1908   1993

Important Dates

1933 Receives law degree from Howard University

1940 Wins first case before the Supreme Court

1954 Wins case called Brown v. Board of Education of Topeka

1991 Retires from the Supreme Court

Our World Neighbors

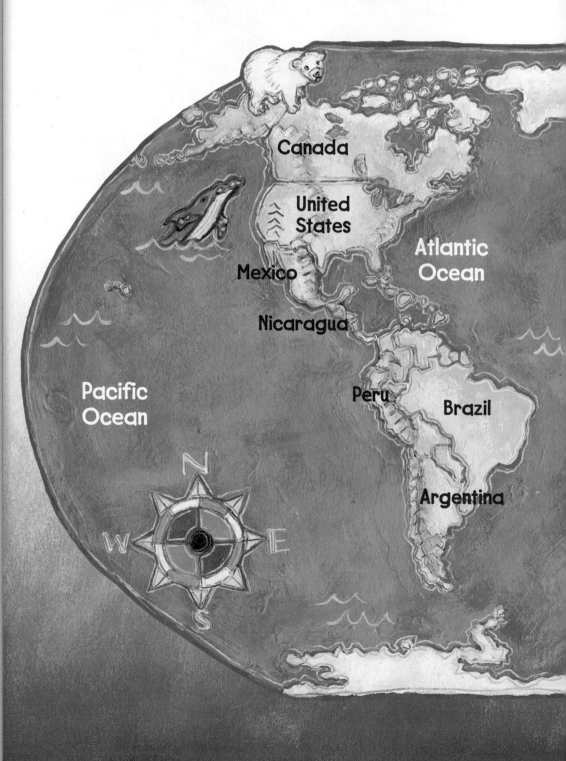

Canada

United States

Mexico

Nicaragua

Atlantic Ocean

Pacific Ocean

Peru

Brazil

Argentina

N
E
S
W

The world is made up of many **nations**, or countries. Each nation has its own government and laws. The United States is a nation. Mexico and Canada are nations that share borders with the United States.

There are more than 190 nations in the world.

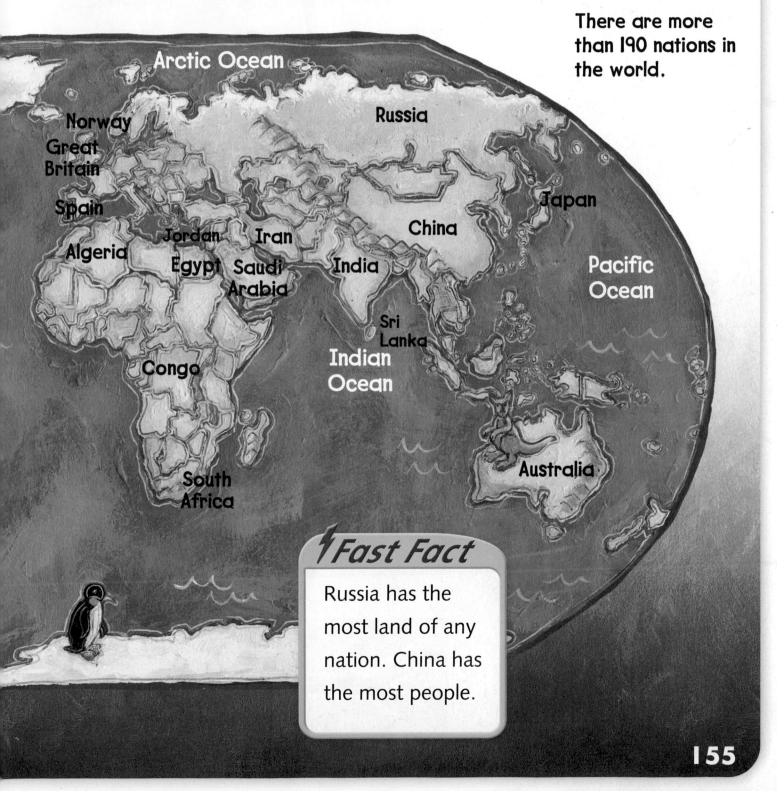

Arctic Ocean

Norway
Great
Britain

Russia

Spain

Japan

Jordan   Iran   China
Algeria
Egypt Saudi   India
Arabia

Pacific
Ocean

Sri
Lanka

Congo

Indian
Ocean

Australia

South
Africa

⚡*Fast Fact*

Russia has the most land of any nation. China has the most people.

In different nations, people become leaders in different ways. In some nations, leaders are chosen by citizens in elections. In other nations, people become leaders by winning wars.

The leaders of some nations are born into families of leaders. They grow up to take the place of their parents as leaders.

King Abdullah II of Jordan

President Chandrika Kumaratunga of Sri Lanka

President Thabo Mbeki of South Africa

Nations also have their own ways of making laws. Some laws come from ways of the culture. Some laws come from the religion of the nation's people. The leaders make sure that the laws are carried out.

House of Lords, England

Summary There are many nations, and each has its own government and laws.

Review

1. 💡 How do other nations make their laws?

2. **Vocabulary** In what **nation** do you live?

3. ✏️ **Write** Choose a nation from the map on pages 154 and 155. Find out how that country makes its laws. Write a paragraph about what you learned.

4. ⭐(Focus Skill) **Main Idea and Details** What are some ways in which people become leaders of other nations?

What to Know
What are some things nations do to get along with one another?

✓ Nations depend on each other for many things.

✓ Nations find ways to get along.

Vocabulary
treaty
ambassador
embassy

Main Idea and Details

California Standards
HSS 2.3.2

Working Together Around the World

Nations have different cultures and different kinds of governments. For many reasons, however, they need to get along with one another.

Sending food

For example, one country might grow food that another country does not have. The other country might make computers that the first country wants. Each can give the other nation what it wants. Nations can also help one another in times of trouble.

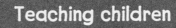

Nations work together to help one another.

Teaching children

Helping after an earthquake

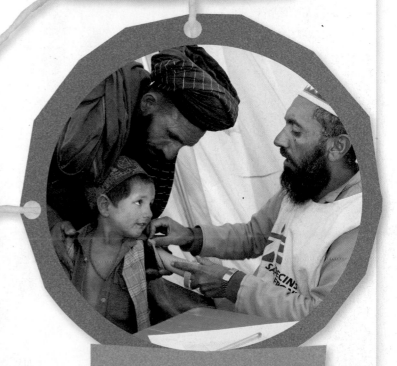

Giving medicine

Sharing Cultures and Ideas

Nations share parts of their cultures, such as their art, music, and writing, with the rest of the world. Nations also share ideas. Men and women of different countries work together to make new discoveries.

Music from Mexico

Dance from Africa

Astronauts from many nations

International Space Station

Members and guests of the United Nations speak different languages. Each member wears earphones to hear the words of other members in his or her own language.

UNITED STATES

UNITED NATIONS

Keeping the Peace

Nations of the world do not always agree on things. They talk about their differences and try to reach agreements that are fair. They might write a **treaty**, or a set of rules that nations agree to follow. Peace treaties keep countries around the world from going to war.

Sometimes nations use ambassadors to help make agreements between their governments. An **ambassador** is a person who speaks and acts for his or her government in another country. He or she lives and works in an **embassy** there. The United States has ambassadors in embassies all over the world. Many nations have embassies here in the United States.

Embassy Row in Washington, D.C.

World leaders meet to discuss problems.

Summary Nations of the world find ways to get along.

Review

1. What are some things nations do to get along with one another?

2. **Vocabulary** What is a **treaty**?

3. **Writing** Imagine that you are the leader of a nation. Write ways in which your nation can get along with other nations.

4. **Main Idea and Details** What are some ways nations work together?

Solve a Problem

❿ Why It Matters

Like leaders of nations, citizens in communities **cooperate**, or work together, to solve problems. A **problem** is something that is making things difficult.

❿ What You Need to Know

A **solution** is a way to solve a problem. There are steps you can follow to solve a problem.

Step 1 Name the problem.

Step 2 Gather information.

Step 3 Think about different solutions.

Step 4 Think about consequences.

Step 5 Try a solution.

Step 6 Think about how well the solution worked.

❱ Practice the Skill

Look at the picture. Name the problem that needs to be solved. Make a list of possible solutions.

❱ Apply What You Learned

Choose the solution you think is best. Write a paragraph telling what the problem is and why you think the solution you chose will work.

Points of View

The Sidewalk Reporter asks:

"What do you do to get along with your neighbors?"

Amanda

"I clean up after my dog."

Mr. Kim

"I keep my home and yard neat."

View from the Past

Anyokah: Getting Along

In 1817, six-year-old Anyokah began working with her father, Sequoyah, to help the people of her community get along. By 1821, they had created an alphabet for the Cherokee people.

Josh

"I drive slowly and watch for people."

Mrs. Avila

"I work on the city council."

Elena

"I don't litter. I use trash cans in the park."

ANALYSIS SKILL

It's Your Turn

- Do you do any of the things that these citizens do? If so, which ones?
- What do you do to get along with your neighbors? What laws do you follow?

The Bundle of Sticks

A Fable by Aesop

illustrated by Laurence Cleyet-Merle

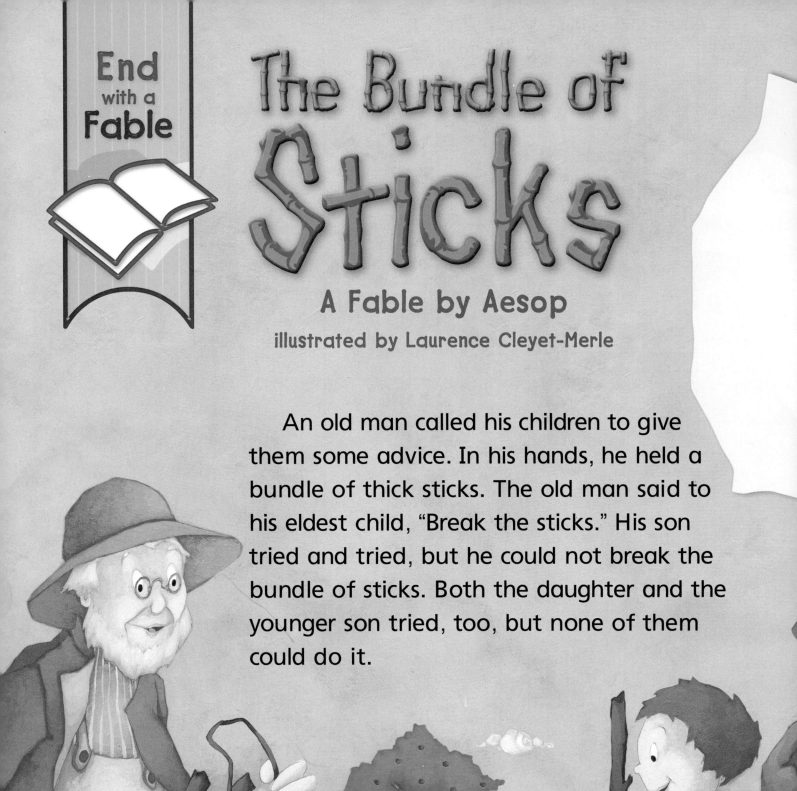

An old man called his children to give them some advice. In his hands, he held a bundle of thick sticks. The old man said to his eldest child, "Break the sticks." His son tried and tried, but he could not break the bundle of sticks. Both the daughter and the younger son tried, too, but none of them could do it.

"Look," said the old man. "Untie the bundle, and each of you take a stick." When they had done this, the old man called out to them, "Now break." Each stick was easily broken. "You see my meaning," he said.

MORAL: Working together, we are strong.

Response Corner

What makes our country strong?

Yerba Buena Gardens

Get Ready

Visitors to San Francisco—and the people who live there—enjoy visiting Yerba Buena Gardens. This place is more than a garden. There are also theaters, museums, a bowling center, a playground, an ice-skating rink, and much more. There is something for everyone at the Yerba Buena Gardens!

Locate It
California

San Francisco

What to See

Children learn how to make animated videos at the Zeum.

This waterfall is part of the Martin Luther King, Jr., Memorial.

There are many kinds of art to see in the San Francisco Museum of Modern Art.

People can enjoy dance, music, and plays at the Yerba Buena Center for the Arts.

At the Rooftop, children can ride the carousel.

A Virtual Tour

GO ONLINE

Visit VIRTUAL TOURS at
www.harcourtschool.com/hss

171

Government A government makes laws to maintain order and help people get along.

Focus Skill Main Idea and Details

Copy and fill in the Main Idea and Details chart to show what you learned about what government does.

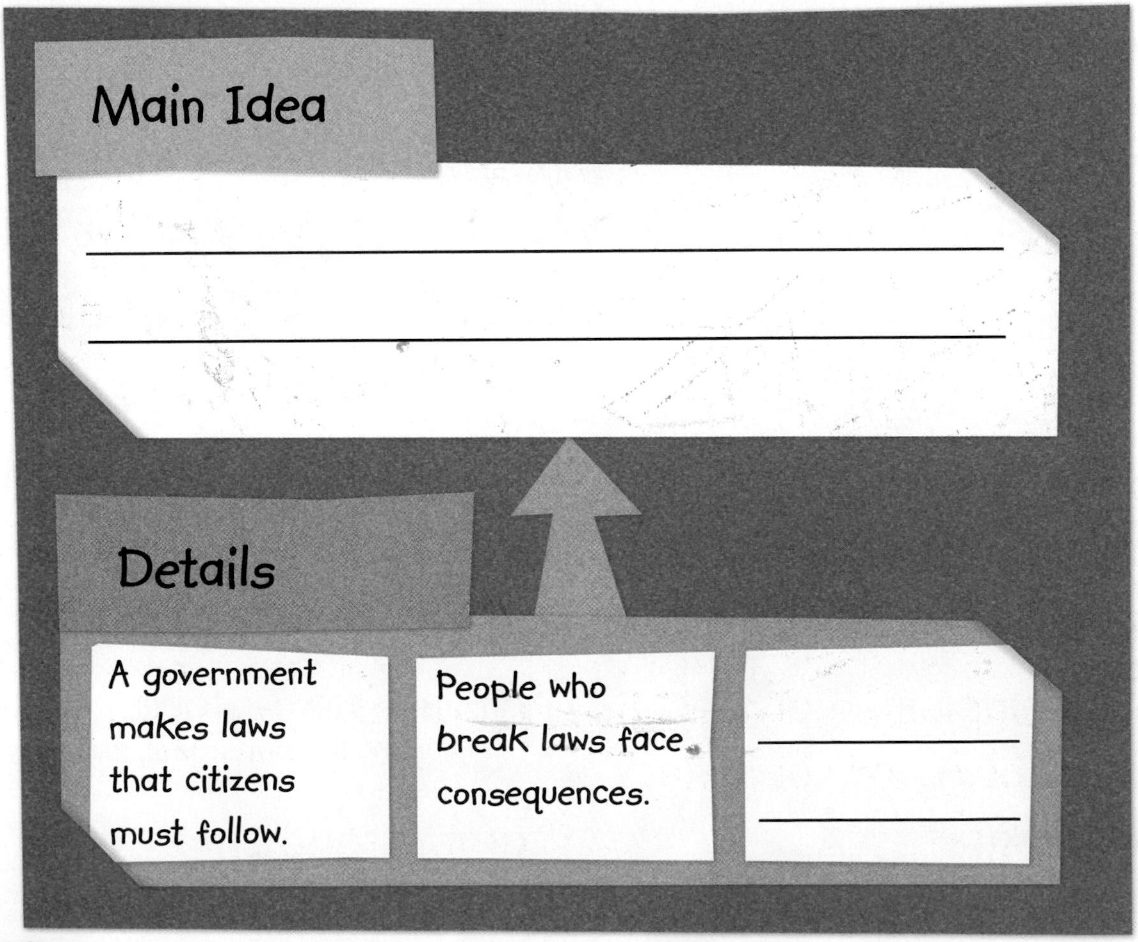

Main Idea

_____

_____

Details

| A government makes laws that citizens must follow. | People who break laws face consequences. | _____ _____ |

Use Vocabulary

Fill in the blanks with the correct words.

My neighbor, Mrs. Arnold, likes to
① _____ in elections. By voting, she
helps choose the people who run our
community. This group of people, called a
② _____, helps everyone get along.
Mrs. Arnold is a good **③** _____ in our
community. She follows every **④** _____,
or rule. I think she could someday be our
country's **⑤** _____ and keep it a good
place to live.

citizen
(p. 132)
government
(p. 136)
law
(p. 136)
President
(p. 147)
vote
(p. 150)

Recall Facts

⑥ What kinds of freedoms do Americans have?

⑦ What is the job of a judge?

⑧ What are some ways people in other nations become leaders?

⑨ How many judges are on the Supreme Court?

    A 5   **C** 12

    B 9   **D** 10

⑩ Who helps make agreements between governments of countries?

    A Congress   **C** ambassador

    B Supreme Court   **D** President

Think Critically

⓫ **ANALYSIS SKILL** Why do you think new laws have to be added to the Constitution?

⓬ **Make It Relevant** What would happen if there were no consequences for breaking laws in your community?

Apply Map and Globe Skills

Western United States

⓭ What is the capital city of New Mexico?

⓮ What states share a border with Washington?

⓯ Of what state is Salem the capital?

⓰ What is the capital city of Idaho?

Apply Participation Skills

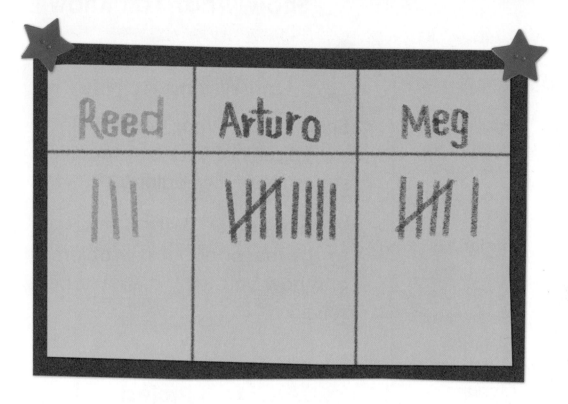

⑰ Who has the least amount of votes?

⑱ How many votes does Meg have?

⑲ How many votes does Arturo have?

⑳ Who has the majority of votes?

Unit 3 Activities

Read More

Working Together to Save Our Planet
by Jeri Cipriano

We Elect a President
by Jeri Cipriano

Leaders for Peace
by Dan Ahearn

Show What You Know

Unit Writing Activity

Speak Out! What would help the citizens of your community stay safe and get along?

Write a Letter Write a letter to the mayor about a problem and how you think it should be solved.

Unit Project

Role Play Role-play how a city council makes laws.

- Practice presenting opinions.
- Use props and simple costumes.
- Role-play a council meeting and write a new law.

GO ONLINE Visit ACTIVITIES at www.harcourtschool.com/hss

176

Using Our Resources

Start with the Standards

2.4 Students understand basic economic concepts and their individual roles in the economy and demonstrate basic economic reasoning skills.

The Big Idea

Resources

People have always needed the land and its resources in order to live.

What to Know

✔ What is a natural resource?

✔ How did people get their food long ago?

✔ How do farmers of today use technology to produce food?

✔ How does food get from the farm to our tables?

Show What You Know

★ Unit 4 Test

✎ Writing: A Descriptive Paragraph

🖌 Unit Project: An Earth Resource Flowchart

Using Our Resources

Talk About

Resources

" We grow our food in the rich California soil. "

"Our neighborhood market sells fresh fruits and vegetables."

"Water is also an important resource."

177

Vocabulary

natural resource Something found in nature that people use.

(page 188)

technology The use of new objects and ideas in everyday life.

(page 202)

raw material A resource used to make a product. (page 212)

product Something that is made by nature or by people. (page 208)

GO ONLINE

INTERNET RESOURCES
Go to **www.harcourtschool.com/hss** to view Internet resources for this unit.

Reading Social Studies

Focus Skill
Cause and Effect

As you read, it can be helpful to know why things happen.

- What makes something happen is a **cause**.
- What happens is the **effect**.

Practice the Skill

Read the following paragraph.

Effect
Cause

Green beans come from bean plants. I grew my own beans! I filled a cup with soil. I pressed bean seeds into the soil and waited. The seeds did not grow because I forgot to water them. Then I watered my seeds carefully. They began to grow. When the bean plants got bigger, I planted them outside.

Apply What You Learned

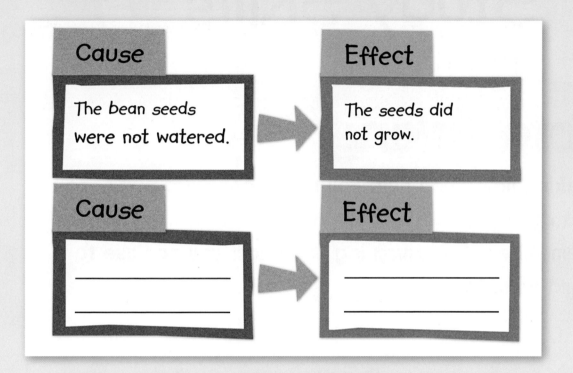

Cause		Effect
The bean seeds were not watered.	→	The seeds did not grow.
Cause		Effect
_____ _____	→	_____ _____

This chart shows what happened to the seeds and why it happened. What can you add to the chart? Copy the chart and complete it.

Apply as You Read

As you read this unit, look for the ways people got their food long ago. Look for ways they get their food today. What has changed? Find out what caused these changes.

Note Taking

Taking notes can help you remember what you read. Notes are important words and sentences that you want to remember. A learning log is a chart you can use to record your notes.

Practice the Skill

Kevin took notes about the paragraph shown on the next page. He wrote his notes in a learning log.

- He wrote words and sentences from the paragraph under Note Taking.

- He wrote his own ideas and thoughts under Note Making.

Learning Log

Note Taking	Note Making
Banana farms are called plantations.	It is too cold to grow bananas where I live.
Weather must be hot and wet.	Green bananas are hard. I don't like how they taste!
_____	_____
_____	_____

Read the paragraph below. Add your own notes to the learning log.

Bananas grow on large farms called plantations. The weather must be very hot and wet. Bananas are picked when they are green and kept in special rooms until they turn yellow. Then they are sold in stores.

Apply as You Read

Make a learning log to help you take notes about using our resources. As you read this unit, add notes to help you remember what you learn.

183

THE TORTILLA FACTORY

by Gary Paulsen
illustrated by Ruth Wright Paulsen

The black earth sleeps
in winter.
But in the spring the
black earth is worked by
brown hands that plant
yellow seeds, which become
green plants rustling in
soft wind and make golden
corn to dry in hot sun and
be ground into flour

184

for the tortilla factory,
where laughing people
and clank-clunking
machinery mix the flour
into dough,
and push the dough,
and squeeze the dough,
and flatten the dough...

...and bake the dough
into perfect disks that
come off the machine
and into a package
and onto a truck and
into a kitchen

to be wrapped around juicy beans
and eaten by white teeth, to fill a round stomach
and give strength to the brown hands
that work the black earth
to plant yellow seeds,

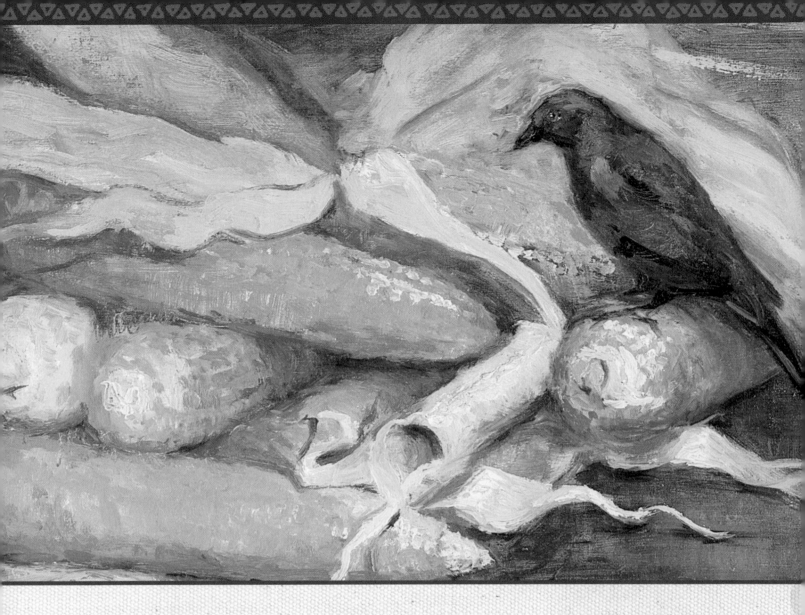

which make golden corn to be dried
in hot sun and be ground into flour...

Response Corner

1. What resources are used
   to make a tortilla?

2. **Make It Relevant** How
   do farmers help you?

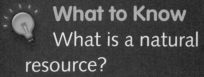
What to Know
What is a natural resource?

✓ People use natural resources to help them live.

✓ It is important to take care of our natural resources.

Vocabulary
natural resource
fuel
conservation

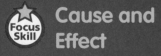 **Focus Skill** Cause and Effect

 California Standards
HSS 2.4, 2.4.1

Land and Water Resources

People need natural resources to live. A **natural resource** is something found in nature that people can use. Air, water, and land are important natural resources.

People Use Air

People, plants, and animals need clean air to live. Some people use moving air to bring power to their homes. A wind turbine uses the wind's energy to produce electricity.

(Reading Check) How do people use air?

People Use Water

People use water in many ways. They use it for drinking, cooking, cleaning, and growing plants for food. Like air, water can also be used to produce electricity. Water produces electricity by flowing through and turning big machines in some dams.

O'Shaughnessy Dam, Yosemite, California

Reading Check How do people use water?

wind turbines

People Use Land

Another natural resource is land. We grow plants for food and build houses on land.

Trees are a very useful natural resource. Some farmers grow trees that make fruits and nuts. Wood from other kinds of trees is used to make furniture and build homes. People also use wood to make paper.

Under the ground, people find other natural resources, such as coal, oil, and natural gas. People dig and drill for these resources and make them into fuel. A **fuel** is a resource that can be burned for heat or energy.

Reading Check How do people use land?

Caring for Our Resources

With so many people living on Earth, we must find ways to protect our resources. One way is by conservation. **Conservation** is the saving of resources to make them last longer. Recycling is another way to save resources. When we recycle, we use something again in a new way.

Communities help care for resources by recycling.

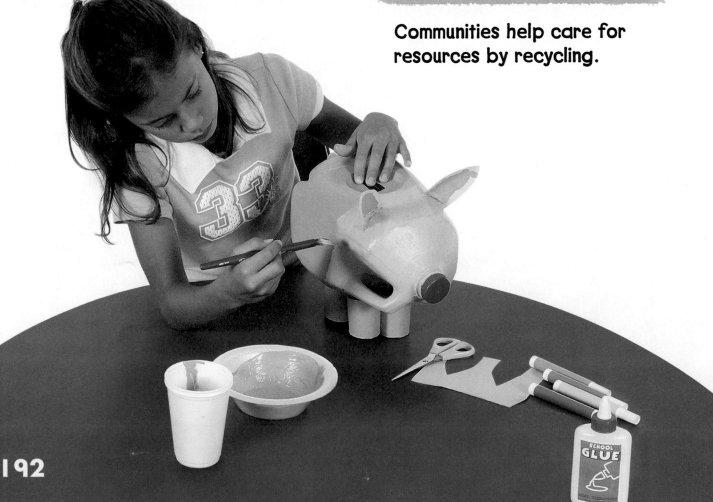

If we don't take care of our natural resources, they can become dirty. Anything that makes the air, land, or water dirty is called pollution. Clean air, water, and land help all living things stay healthy.

Reading Check How does conservation help protect our resources?

Summary Natural resources give us what we need to live.

Recycling food garbage can keep soil healthy.

Review

1. 💡 What is a natural resource?

2. **Vocabulary** What are two kinds of **fuel**?

3. ✏️ **Write** Keep a natural resource log. Write down all of the resources you use in one day.

4. ⭐ (Focus Skill) **Cause and Effect** Why should we take care of our natural resources?

What to Know
How did people get their food long ago?

✓ Pioneer families used climate to decide when to plant and harvest crops.

✓ Everyone in a pioneer family worked hard to grow and prepare food.

Vocabulary
crop
climate

Focus Skill Cause and Effect

California Standards
HSS 2.4.1

Getting Food Long Ago

Many pioneers made their homes on farms. They used their land and water to grow crops to feed their families. **Crops** are plants that people grow for food or other needs.

Growing Seasons

The growing season in California can be long or short, depending on a place's climate. **Climate** is the kind of weather a place has over time. In the Central Valley, the climate is hot and dry in the summer. It is mild and wet in the winter. This climate is good for growing wheat, so many farmers there grew this crop.

In the spring, the farmer plowed the fields. The plow made rows in the soil. Women and children helped plant seeds in the rows. The farmer then covered the seeds with more soil.

During the summer, everyone watched over their crops. They scared away animals and birds that wanted to eat the plants.

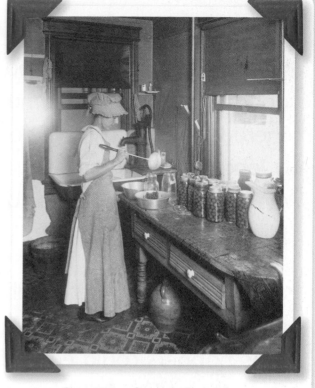

Storing food for the winter in 1910.

The farmers harvested, or gathered, their crops in the fall. They sold some of the food, but they kept most of it for the family to eat during the winter.

(Reading Check) What effect did climate have on pioneer farmers?

Problems with Crops

Pioneer farmers worried about weather. Sometimes, there would be no rain for a long time, and crops would die. Bad storms could also kill plants.

Farmers also worried about insects and other hungry animals. Large swarms of grasshoppers could eat a farmer's whole crop in a single day. Rabbits and mice often ate the young plants as soon as they began to grow.

When crops were ruined, some pioneer families gave up and went back to where they had once lived. Other families stayed where they were and started over.

Reading Check What might ruin a farmer's crops?

Summary Long ago, people worked hard to grow the food they needed.

Review

1. How did people get their food long ago?

2. **Vocabulary** Name a job that a farmer did to grow a **crop**.

3. **Activity** Draw a picture that shows how a farmer of long ago got food from the land.

4. **Cause and Effect** Why might pioneer families move back to where they had lived?

Tools Long Ago

People who study history are called historians. Historians look at objects that people used long ago. This helps them learn how the people lived and what tools they used to meet their needs.

"OUR FIELD IS THE WORLD."

LIGHT DRAFT, SUPERIOR DESIGN.

CLEAN AND RAPID CUTTER.

McCormick Harvesting Machine Co., Chicago.

ESTABLISHED 1831.

❶ Farmers from long ago used these tools on their farms.

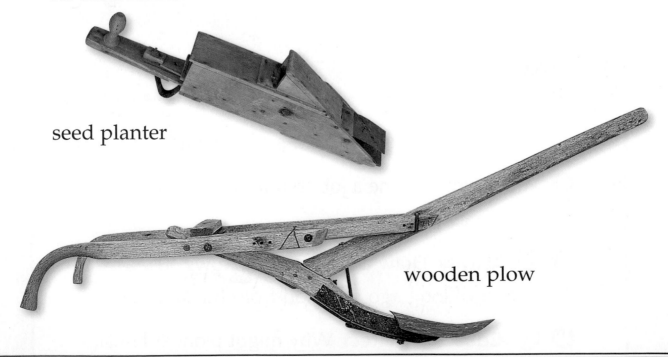

seed planter

wooden plow

Farmers could buy their
tools from a catalog.

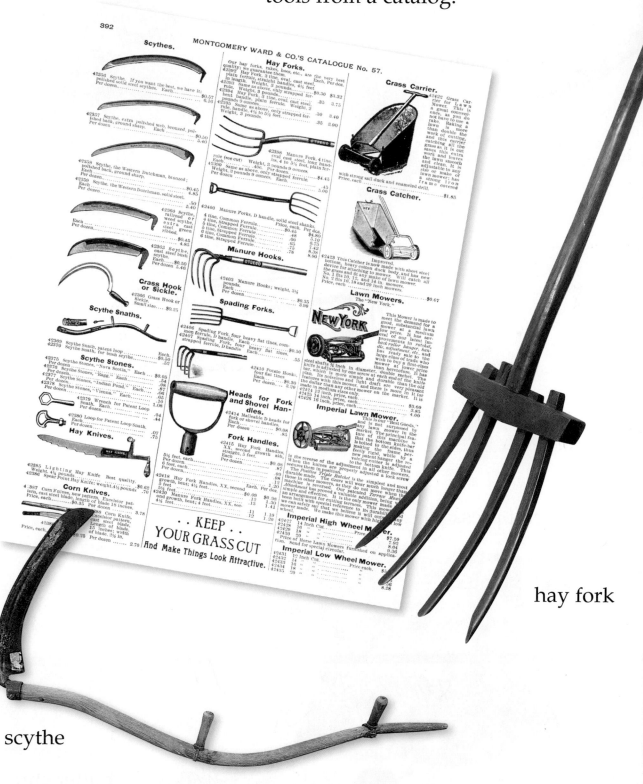

scythe

hay fork

② People long ago also needed tools to help them prepare and eat the food they grew.

food masher

biscuit cutter

toaster

fruit press

butter churn

Gathering buffalo chips for fuel

Getting water

 Analyze Primary Sources

Look again at the tools people used to prepare food long ago. Which tools have changed? How have they changed? Write a paragraph describing how a tool has changed.

Visit PRIMARY SOURCES at
www.harcourtschool.com/hss

Lesson 3

Farming Today

What to Know
How do farmers of today use technology to produce food?

- Technology has changed the way farmers do their work.

- New tools help today's farmers grow larger crops than farmers of long ago could.

Vocabulary
technology

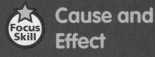
Cause and Effect

California Standards
HSS 2.4.1

Many of the tools that farmers use today are different from the ones farmers used long ago. Technology has made farm work easier and faster. **Technology** is the use of new objects and ideas in everyday life.

ANALYSIS SKILL How has planting seeds changed?

Technology and Farming

Technology helps farmers of today grow larger crops than farmers of the past could grow. Work that once took a week can now be done in a few hours. Farmers can now plant and harvest crops on more land in the same amount of time. This means that present-day farmers can produce much more food.

Better farming tools help farmers with their work. A disc breaks up the soil before planting. A cultivator loosens the soil around the roots of the plants so water can easily get to them. A harvester cuts wheat and takes out the wheat kernels.

How do these farming tools help farmers with their crops?

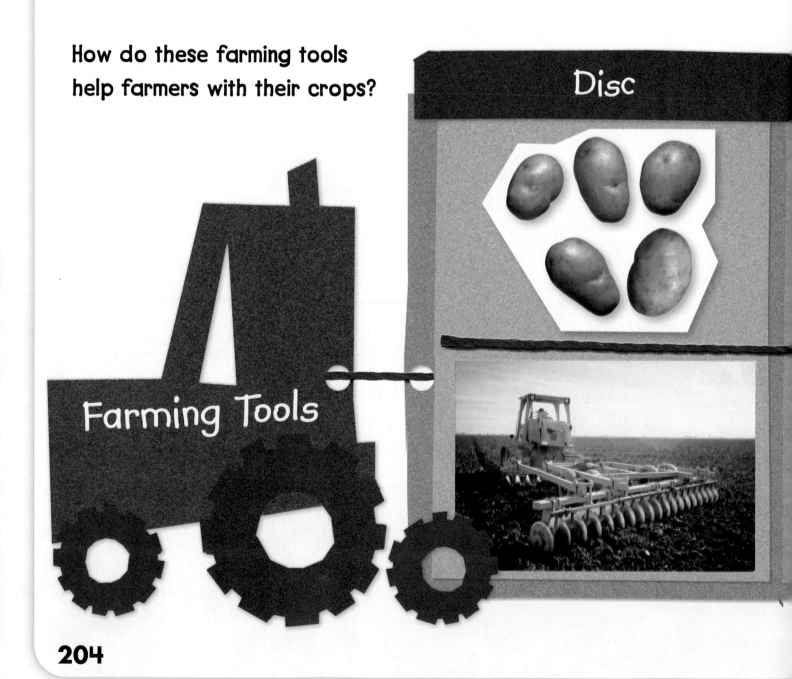

Farming Tools

Disc

Making sure crops get enough water is important. In places with a dry climate, many farmers use pipes and sprayers to bring water to crops.

Reading Check What are some of the tools that farmers use today?

Cultivator

Harvester

Future Farming

In the future, farming may use less of one natural resource. Hydroponics is a kind of farming that does not use soil. Plants grow in water that has the minerals in it that they need. Pumps move air and water around the roots.

What natural resources does hydroponics use? What resource does it save?

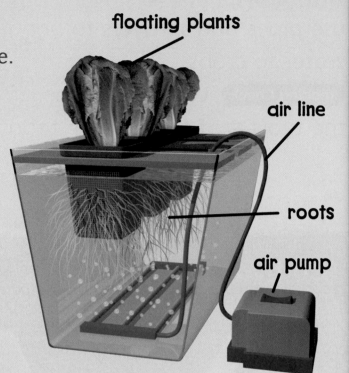

floating plants

air line

roots

air pump

Technology and Weather

New technology can also help farmers know what kind of weather is coming. Farmers get information about temperature, wind, moisture, and storms. This helps them know the best times to plant and harvest their crops.

Radar image of the weather in the Los Angeles area

Reading Check How does new technology help farmers know what the weather will be like?

Summary New technology helps farmers grow and produce more food than farmers of the past could grow.

Review

1. How do farmers of today use technology to produce food?

2. **Vocabulary** Name one kind of **technology** farmers use.

3. **Activity** Draw a picture of a farm tool of today. Explain how it helps farmers.

4. **Cause and Effect** What effect has new technology had on farming?

Read a Product Map

▶ Why It Matters

Some maps show the resources and products of a place. A **product** is something that is made by nature or by people.

▶ What You Need to Know

A **product map** uses symbols to identify resources and products and shows where they are found or made. This map shows some of the resources and products of California.

▶ Practice the Skill

❶ What products are shown in the map legend?

❷ Which animal is raised in southern California?

❸ In which body of water are fish located?

❹ Where in California are forest products found?

California Products

Map Legend
- Beef cattle
- Cotton
- Dairy products
- Fish
- Forest products
- Grapes
- Other fruits

OREGON

NEVADA

Klamath River

Eureka

Redding

Sacramento River

Lake Tahoe

Santa Rosa

Sacramento

Stockton

Oakland

San Francisco

Modesto

San Jose

San Joaquin R.

Monterey

Salinas River

Fresno

Ridgecrest

Mojave Desert

Bakersfield

Barstow

Needles

PACIFIC OCEAN

North

West — East

South

Santa Barbara

Los Angeles

Pasadena

Palm Springs

Salton Sea

Long Beach

Colorado River

ARIZONA

Escondido

San Diego

MEXICO

0   75   150 Miles
0   75   150 Kilometers

❯ Apply What You Learned

ANALYSIS SKILL Rice is another crop grown in California. Find out where rice is grown. Where would a symbol for it go on the map?

 Practice your map and globe skills with the **GeoSkills CD-ROM**.

The Edible Schoolyard

Alice Waters and school children

Farmers know how important good soil is to growing food. Read about a woman who wants children to learn what farmers know by learning how to grow their own food.

Alice Waters thought people did not know enough about eating and growing healthful food. At a school in California, she worked with people in the community to start a garden.

The garden is a way for children to learn how food is grown. Children choose from jobs like pulling weeds or planting seeds. They write in their garden journals about their jobs and what they learn.

The Edible Schoolyard Project at Martin Luther King, Jr., Middle School in Berkeley, California

210

The school later added a kitchen classroom. There, children work together to make meals with food from their garden.

After they make the meals, the children get to eat. They sit and talk and eat in calm surroundings, just as Alice Waters believes people should eat their food.

Did You Know?

Did you know that you can do things to show that you care about your school?

★ Ask if you can plant a flower garden for everyone to enjoy.

★ Put all trash where it goes.

Think About It!

Make It Relevant
What should a good citizen learn about the land?

From Farm to Table

What to Know
How does food get from the farm to our tables?

✔ Farmers send their crops to processing plants.

✔ Distributors get the food to the markets.

Vocabulary
raw material
market
processing plant
distributor

 Focus Skill Cause and Effect

California Standards
HSS 2.4.1

The Cavazos family owns an orange grove, or farm, in California. The oranges are **raw materials**, or resources used to make a product. The Cavazoses sell some of their oranges to markets. A **market** is a place that sells food. They also sell oranges to places where oranges are made into juice.

At the Farm

Many people are needed to pick the ripe oranges. The Cavazos family hires migrant workers to help. Migrant workers go from farm to farm.

Some years ago, migrant workers were treated unfairly. A man named Cesar Chavez helped migrant workers in California. He started a group now called the United Farm Workers of America. Today, this group makes sure that migrant workers are treated fairly.

Reading Check What did Cesar Chavez do for migrant workers?

Cesar Chavez talking to farm workers about their rights

To the Processing Plant

After the fruit is picked, the oranges are sent to a processing plant. A **processing plant** is a place where food is turned into food products. In this one, oranges are turned into orange juice.

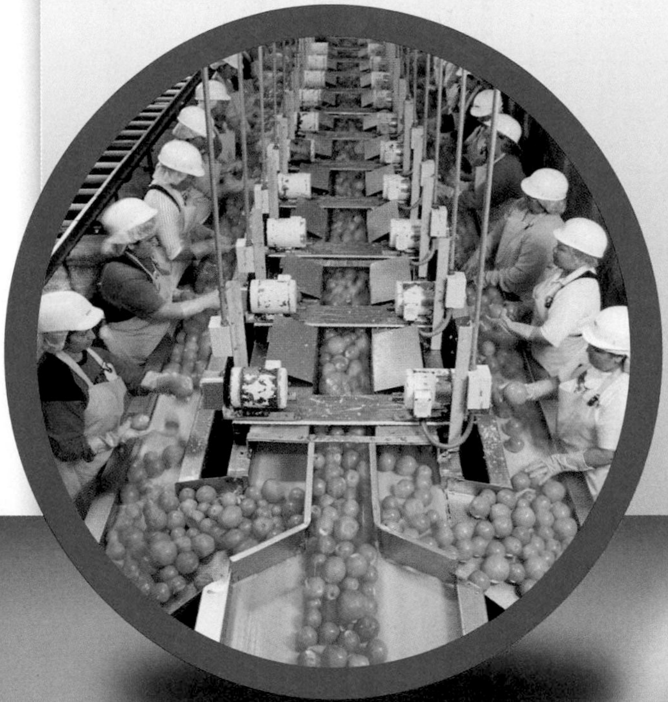

1 Washing

2 Juicing

At the processing plant, the oranges are first washed and sorted. Next, the juice is squeezed from the oranges. Then, the orange juice is heated to make it safe to drink. Last, it is poured into plastic bottles to be sold.

Reading Check How is food changed at the processing plant?

3 Heating

4 Bottling

To the Market

The orange juice is finally ready for markets. A **distributor** takes a food product from the processing plant to the markets.

Food is moved to markets in many ways. Trains or large trucks might deliver the orange juice to places around the United States. Oranges and juice might be sent to another country on a ship or an airplane. All of these kinds of transportation are refrigerated to keep the food fresh.

Food distributors make it possible for farmers like the Cavazoses to get food from their farm to the markets. Then people everywhere can enjoy orange juice from oranges grown in California.

Reading Check What happens to food crops after they are processed?

Summary A crop goes through many steps at different places before it becomes food on the table.

Review

1. 💡 How does food get from the farm to our tables?

2. **Vocabulary** How does a **distributor** take food to markets?

3. ✏️ **Write** Find out how milk gets from the farm to your table. Then write about it. Share the information you found.

4. ⭐ (Focus Skill) **Cause and Effect** Why do distributors refrigerate certain foods as they are shipped? What might happen if they did not?

Use a Flowchart

❯ Why It Matters

A **flowchart** shows the steps needed to make or do something. You can use a flowchart to show the steps workers follow to make a product.

❯ What You Need to Know

The title of the flowchart tells what it is about. Each picture has a sentence that tells about the step. Arrows show you the order of the steps.

❯ Practice the Skill

1 What does the flowchart show?

2 What is the first step?

3 What happens after the oranges are processed?

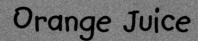

Orange Juice

① The oranges are picked.

② The oranges are processed.

③ The juice is taken to market.

④ The juice is bought at the market.

❱ Apply What You Learned

Make It Relevant   List the steps for something you do every day. Use your list to make a flowchart.

Trustworthiness

Respect

Responsibility

Fairness

Caring

Patriotism

Why Character Counts

❓ **How did Dolores Huerta's responsibility help farmworkers?**

Dolores Huerta

As a teacher, Dolores Huerta saw her students come to school hungry and needing shoes. She decided she could help her students by helping their parents. Many of them were farmworkers from Mexico and did not speak English. Huerta said, "Giving kids clothes and food is one thing, but it's much more important to teach them that other people besides themselves are important . . ."*

*Dolores Huerta. Words of Women Quotations for Success. Power Dynamics Publishing, 1997.

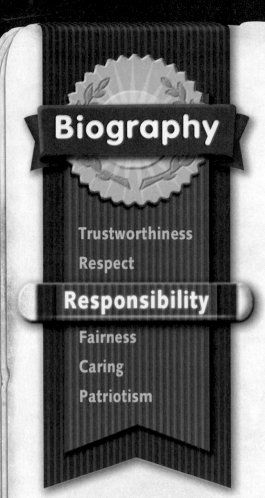

Dolores Huerta worked to get better living conditions for farmworkers.

Posters reminded people to help the farmworkers by not buying certain food.

Dolores Huerta worked with Cesar Chavez to form the National Farm Workers Association.

Bio Brief

| 1930 | Present |

Important Dates

1980s Opens the radio station KUFW to speak for farmworkers

1984 Is given the Outstanding Labor Leader Award

1993 Is honored in the National Women's Hall of Fame

1999 Is given the Presidential Eleanor D. Roosevelt Human Rights Award by President Clinton

Dolores Huerta spoke to many people about the way the farmworkers were mistreated. She asked the people not to buy certain crops. When the farm owners started losing money, they listened to her. In 1975, Huerta's work helped pass the Agricultural Labor Relations Act in California. This act gave farmworkers the right to ask for more pay and better housing.

GO ONLINE

Interactive Multimedia Biographies
Visit MULTIMEDIA BIOGRAPHIES
at **www.harcourtschool.com/hss**

THE STORY OF
Johnny Appleseed

by Aliki

Many years ago
when America was a new country,
there lived a brave and gentle man
named John Chapman.
John loved the out-of-doors.
He would walk for miles
in the woods
among the trees and the flowers,
happy and alone with his thoughts.

One day, after a long walk,
John sat under a tree to rest.
He felt the warm sun on his back,
and the fresh grass tickling his toes.
John took an apple from his sack
and ate it.
And when he had finished,
he looked in his hand
at what was left—
just a few brown seeds.
And John thought:
If one gathered seeds,
and planted them,
our land would soon be filled
with apple trees.

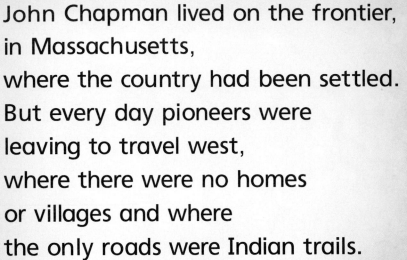

John Chapman lived on the frontier,
in Massachusetts,
where the country had been settled.
But every day pioneers were
leaving to travel west,
where there were no homes
or villages and where
the only roads were Indian trails.

In their covered wagons,
the pioneers made the long
and dangerous journey
through the wilderness.
They wanted to build
new lives for themselves
in a new part of the country.
John Chapman went, too.
But he did not travel in
a covered wagon.
He walked in his bare feet.

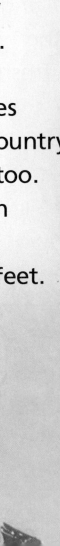

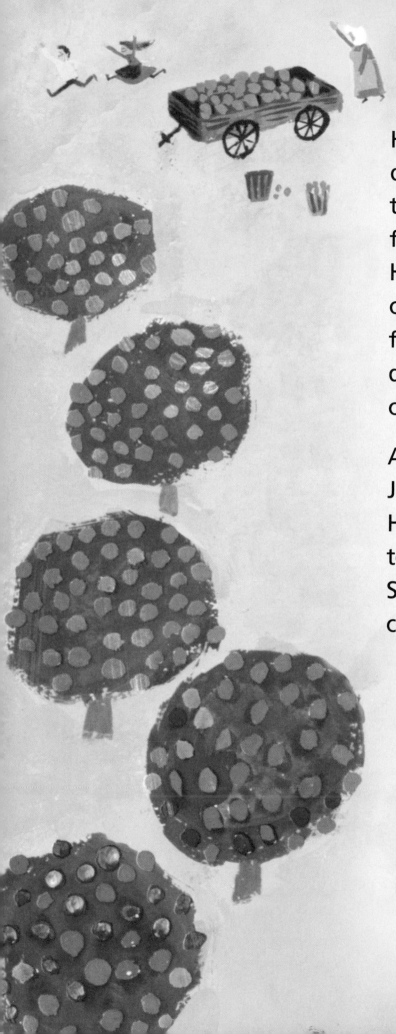

He carried no weapons,
as men did in those days,
to protect themselves
from wild animals and danger.
He carried only a large sack
on his back,
filled with apple seeds,
and his cooking pan
on his head.

As he walked,
John planted seeds.
He gave a small bagful
to everyone he saw.
Soon, everyone who knew him
called him Johnny Appleseed.

Response Corner

What do you think would
have happened if Johnny
Appleseed had not planted
the apple seeds as he walked?

An Abalone Farm

Get Ready

Visitors to the US Abalone farm can see farmers growing a special kind of food. Abalone are mollusks—water animals with a hard outer shell instead of a skeleton. At the farm, the abalone begin as microscopic animals. The farmers sell the abalone to markets when they have grown to be about four inches long. People can then buy them to use as food.

Locate It
California

Davenport Landing

What to See

The US Abalone farm is on Davenport Landing beach. This location lets the farmers pump in the salt water that the abalone need to grow.

The farmers keep the abalone in saltwater tanks. The young feed on algae. After about six months, the farmers move the abalone to different tanks, where they feed them fresh kelp.

It takes four or five years for abalone to be big enough for the farmers to sell them to markets.

A Virtual Tour

GO ONLINE

Visit VIRTUAL TOURS at
www.harcourtschool.com/hss

Review

💡 **Resources** People have always needed the land and its resources in order to live.

⭐ (Focus Skill) **Cause and Effect**

Complete the graphic organizer to show what you have learned about growing crops.

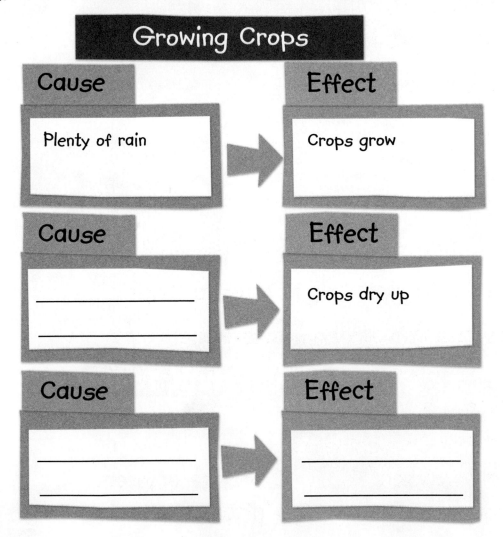

Growing Crops

Cause		Effect
Plenty of rain	→	Crops grow

Cause		Effect
_____ _____	→	Crops dry up

Cause		Effect
_____ _____	→	_____ _____

Use Vocabulary

Complete each sentence.

natural resource
(p. 188)

crop
(p. 194)

technology
(p. 202)

product
(p. 208)

raw materials
(p. 212)

1 Food from the farm is turned into a _____ at the processing plant.

2 New _____, such as tools and machines, helps farmers grow more crops.

3 Oranges are _____ that are used to make other products.

4 Water is an important _____ that some people use to make electricity.

5 Wheat is a kind of _____.

Recall Facts

6 How can people use air as a natural resource?

7 What did a pioneer farmer do in the fall?

8 How do some farmers bring water to crops?

9 Where are oranges turned into orange juice?

    A farm   **C** processing plant

    B home   **D** market

10 Who did Cesar Chavez help?

    A migrant workers   **C** orange growers

    B farmers   **D** distributors

Think Critically

⑪ **ANALYSIS SKILL** Why do different places use their natural resources in different ways?

⑫ **Make It Relevant** What would happen if no one recycled or conserved their resources in your community?

Apply Map and Globe Skills

⑬ What does this map show?

⑭ What products are shown in the map legend?

⑮ Which food crops are grown in the southern part of California?

⑯ Where in California are tomatoes found?

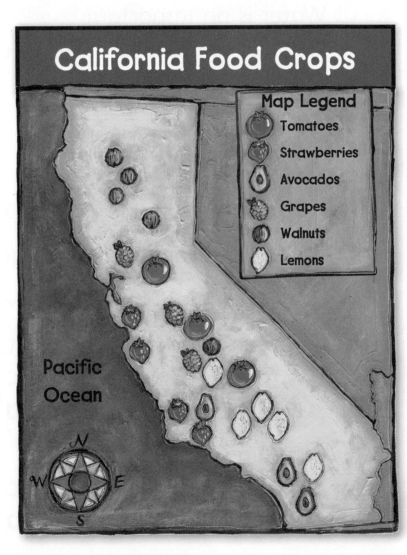

California Food Crops

Map Legend
- Tomatoes
- Strawberries
- Avocados
- Grapes
- Walnuts
- Lemons

Pacific Ocean

Apply Chart and Graph Skills

Recycling

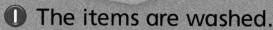

1 The items are washed.

2 The items are sorted into bins.

3 The bins are put on the curb.

4 The items are taken away.

17 What does the flowchart show?

18 What is the second step?

19 What happens after the materials are sorted into bins?

20 What happens after the bins are placed at the curb?

Read More

Goods Around the World by Susan Ring

California Raisins by Jordan Brown

From Farm to Table by Lisa deMauro

Show What You Know

Unit Writing Activity

Choose a Product Think about your favorite farm product.

Write a Descriptive Paragraph Write a paragraph describing your favorite farm product. Include facts and details.

Unit Project

Earth Resource Flowchart Create a flowchart about using resources to produce food.

- Brainstorm steps for the flowchart.
- Illustrate and explain a flowchart step.
- Answer questions for guests.

GO ONLINE Visit ACTIVITIES at www.harcourtschool.com/hss

People in the Marketplace

The Big Idea

Work

Producers and consumers depend on each other for the goods and services they want. Producers provide the goods and services that consumers buy.

What to Know

✔ How do producers and consumers depend on each other?

✔ How do people get money to pay for goods and services?

✔ Why do we make, sell, and buy more of some things than others?

✔ Why do countries trade goods with other countries?

Show What You Know

★ Unit 5 Test

✎ Writing: An Advertisement

🖌 Unit Project: A Class Fair

People in the Marketplace

Talk About

Work

"I earned money to buy a gift for my brother."

"I think about the cost before I choose what I will buy."

"I use money I saved to buy what I want."

233

producer   A person who grows, makes, or sells goods. (page 246)

goods   Things that can be bought and sold. (page 247)

services   Work done for others. (page 247)

consumer   A person who buys and uses goods and services. (page 249)

marketplace   Where people buy and sell goods and services. (page 270)

GO ONLINE   INTERNET RESOURCES
Go to **www.harcourtschool.com/hss** to view Internet resources for this unit.

235

Reading Social Studies

★ Focus Skill Categorize and Classify

As you read, you can categorize and classify information. When you categorize and classify, you sort things into groups.

● Decide what each group will be called.

● Place each thing in a group.

Practice the Skill

Read the following paragraph.

Categorize
Classify

Rob and Mom shopped at the Farmers' Market. They bought fresh food, plants, and toys. The foods they bought were peppers and cucumbers. Mom chose a yellow rosebush and daisies for the garden. Rob bought some toys—a wooden whistle and a puzzle. At the end of the day, Mom bought a cup of lemonade and Rob bought grape juice. They had fun on their shopping trip!

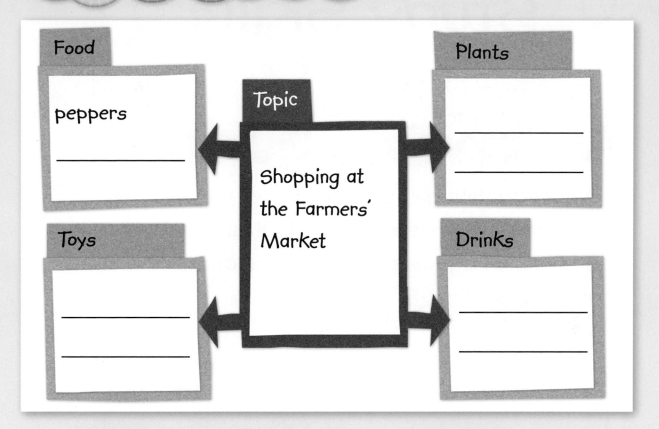

Food

peppers

_____

Plants

_____

_____

Toys

_____

_____

Topic

Shopping at the Farmers' Market

Drinks

_____

_____

Use this chart to categorize and classify the things that Rob and Mom bought. Some are foods. Some are not. What else did Rob and Mom buy? Copy the chart and complete it.

Apply as You Read

As you read this unit, look for ways to categorize and classify information.

Anticipation Guide

An anticipation guide helps you get ready to read. An anticipation guide is a list of statements. As you read, you will discover whether the statements are true or false.

Practice the Skill

Copy the statements on the next page. Work in a small group to decide what you think about each one.

- Read each statement.

- Circle T if you think the statement is correct.

- Circle F if you think the statement is incorrect.

Anticipation Guide

T	F	1. People usually make all of the things they need.
T	F	2. Most people do not need to earn money to buy what they want.
T	F	3. People cannot own their own businesses.
T	F	4. If everyone wants to buy the same item, it can be hard to find.
T	F	5. Sometimes you have to save to buy things you want.
T	F	6. Every country has all the resources it needs.

Apply as You Read

Use the anticipation guide above as you read the unit. Talk about how the information in the unit changed your thoughts about some of the statements.

SUPERMARKET

by Kathleen Krull

illustrated by Melanie Hope Greenberg

Shopping carts clang.
Magic doors whiz open and shut.
Colors glow under bright white lights.
So many breakfasts, lunches, and dinners!
It's all at a special, necessary, very real place:
the supermarket.

OATS & MORE

According to surveys, shoppers decide in their first 8 seconds whether they feel comfortable in a store. The first thing they see helps them decide.

The doors don't really open by magic. When an electronic "eye" overhead "sees" you coming, it starts a motor to open the doors.

The supermarket is a whole world of its own. Where does all this crunchy, munchy, sweet, sour, fiery, frozen, fabulous food come from?

Happy Farms

Certain states are famous for certain foods: Iowa for popcorn, Vermont for maple syrup, Michigan for cereal, Wisconsin for cheese, Idaho for potatoes, Massachusetts for cranberries, Florida for oranges, California for grapes, Georgia for peaches and peanuts.

It all begins on farms. Our food comes from places with lots of sunshine, rich soil, and clean water. Farmers make decisions every day during the long months of growing.

At harvesttime, workers pick the fruits and vegetables. They pack everything neatly in boxes and load the boxes onto trucks.

Picking fruits and vegetables can be painful, low-paying work. Cesar Chavez (1927-1993) became a hero for workers when he founded the National Farm Workers of America.

Small trucks, big trucks, gigantic trucks—
all rev up their engines.
Every night, drivers take off from farms or warehouses.

244

They zoom down the highway toward your town.

Response Corner

1. Interview someone who works at a supermarket to find out how one of your favorite foods gets to the store.

2. **Make It Relevant**   What are some of the foods your family buys?

What to Know
How do producers and consumers depend on each other?

✔ Producers provide goods and services.

✔ Consumers buy goods and services.

Vocabulary
producer
goods
services
business
consumer
factory

Focus Skill **Categorize and Classify**

California Standards
HSS 2.4, 2.4.2

246

Producers and Consumers

Christina and her family live in a community in which people have many kinds of jobs. Some workers grow or make products, and others sell products. A worker who grows, makes, or sells products is called a **producer**.

Goods and Services

Products are also called goods. **Goods** are things that can be bought and sold. Christina's grandmother grows flowers to sell. Her dad makes parts that are used to make computers.

Producers also provide services. **Services** are work people do for others. Dr. Briggs takes care of Christina's teeth. Mr. West teaches her to play the cello.

Reading Check How are goods and services alike?

247

Buying and Selling

Christina and her mom go shopping downtown. Main Street has many businesses. A person who owns a **business** makes or sells goods or provides services. Christina gets her hair cut at the salon. She and her mom buy sandals at the shoe store and raisin bread at the bakery. The salon, the shoe store, and the bakery are all businesses.

Christina and her mom are consumers. A **consumer** is a person who buys goods or services. When consumers buy things, they provide money so producers can buy things. This makes producers consumers, too. The baker buys shoes. The shoe salesperson gets a haircut. The hairstylist buys bread.

Reading Check How can a person be both a consumer and a producer?

Shoe Store

Bakery

Producers at Work

Some goods are grown. Others are made by hand. Many goods we buy in stores are made in factories. A **factory** is a building in which people use machines to make goods.

Christina wants to buy a new bicycle helmet. At the factory, each worker has a special job.

Workers in the factory office order supplies and keep track of payments. Some workers design the helmets. Then they test the helmets to make sure they are safe to use. Other workers make the different parts of the helmet. Then workers put together the different parts. These producers work together so that Christina can be safe when she rides her bicycle down the street.

Reading Check What happens at a factory before a helmet can be sold?

Summary Producers work to provide consumers with goods and services.

Review

1. How do producers and consumers depend on each other?

2. **Vocabulary** Do producers at a **factory** provide goods or services?

3. **Activity** Make a chart that shows some of the goods and services your family buys.

4. **Categorize and Classify** When Christina got her hair cut, did she buy goods or a service?

251

Read a Bar Graph

▶ Why It Matters

Some kinds of information are easier to find in a bar graph. A **bar graph** uses bars to show amounts or numbers of things.

▶ What You Need to Know

A bar graph's title tells you the kind of information it shows. Each bar stands for a different group being counted. You read some bar graphs from left to right and others from bottom to top.

▶ Practice the Skill

❶ How many dogs went to the Pet Palace on Tuesday?

❷ On which day did the Pet Palace groom five dogs?

❸ What were the two busiest days at the Pet Palace?

252

Dogs Groomed at the Pet Palace

	0	1	2	3	4	5	6	7
Sunday								
Monday								
Tuesday								
Wednesday								
Thursday								
Friday								
Saturday								

❯ Apply What You Learned

Make It Relevant   Make a bar graph. Show different kinds of pets and the number of people you know who have each kind.

253

Trustworthiness

Respect
Responsibility
Fairness
Caring
Patriotism

Levi Strauss

Levi Strauss learned from his family to be a good business owner. He knew that people wanted to buy good products at fair prices. When gold was discovered in California, Strauss moved his business west. He wanted to sell dry goods—clothes, blankets, and other supplies—to the miners.

Why Character Counts

❓ **Why was it important that Levi Strauss was trustworthy in his business with others?**

Looking for gold was hard on clothes. The miners asked Levi Strauss for pants that would last a long time.

Levi Strauss was a business owner who helped make jeans.

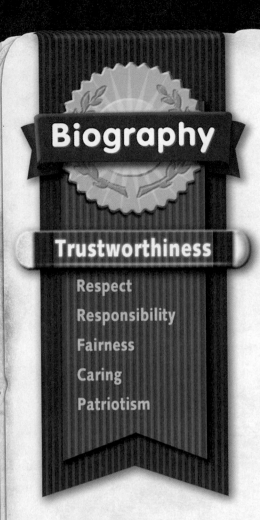

Metal rivets and denim fabric made jeans last longer than other pants.

Hard work and rugged land quickly wore out miners' clothing.

Jacob Davis, a tailor, had the idea that if pockets were attached with metal rivets, they would not tear easily. But Davis did not have enough money to make the pants to sell. Strauss offered to use his own money to make the pants. Then both could make money when they sold the pants. The two became partners, and the first jeans were made.

GO ONLINE

Interactive Multimedia Biographies
Visit MULTIMEDIA BIOGRAPHIES
at **www.harcourtschool.com/hss**

Bio Brief

1829   1902

Important Dates

1853 Becomes a U.S. citizen
Starts business in San Francisco

1872 Applies for U.S. patent for jeans with riveted pockets

1873 With Jacob Davis, gets patent to make jeans on May 20

What to Know

How do people get money to pay for goods and services?

✓ People have different occupations.

✓ People earn income to buy goods and services.

Vocabulary
occupation
income
free enterprise
want

Categorize and Classify

California Standards
HSS 2.4, 2.4.2

Work and Income

Earning Money

People get paid for making or selling goods or for providing services. An **occupation** is a job a person works at to earn money. The money that people earn is called **income**.

People choose occupations in which they can do work they enjoy. Some may be good at singing or teaching. Others may enjoy building things or working with animals. Many people get special training for their jobs.

Reading Check How do people choose their occupations?

Running a Business

Some people have ideas for businesses of their own. A person who likes to make a product might start a new business to sell that product. The freedom to start and run a business to make money is called **free enterprise**.

Children can take part in free enterprise. They can wash cars, rake leaves, care for pets, and sell things they make. These businesses are all forms of free enterprise. The children who do these jobs earn income.

Reading Check What are some ways children can take part in free enterprise?

Children in History

Abraham Lincoln

When Abraham Lincoln was young, he worked on a flatboat on the Ohio River. He pushed the boat with a long pole. Flatboats carried goods to people who wanted them.

Spending Money

People use their income to buy goods and services. They may also save some of it. They use their money to pay for wants. A **want** is something that people would like to have. A home, food, and clothing are wants. Pets, books, and new bicycles are also wants.

People cannot buy everything they want. They have to make a choice about what things are important to them. Most people first buy the goods and services that will keep them safe and comfortable. Then they buy the goods and services that they would like.

Reading Check How do people decide what goods and services to buy?

Summary People work so that they can earn income to buy goods and services.

Review

1. How do people get money to pay for goods and services?

2. **Vocabulary** What do people do with **income**?

3. **Write** Make a list of things you like to do. Choose one that you could do to earn income.

4. **Categorize and Classify** Write down the occupations of family members or adult friends. Circle the ones in which people make goods.

Read a Picture Graph

❯ Why It Matters

Some information is easier to understand when it is shown in a picture graph. A **picture graph** uses pictures to show numbers of things.

❯ What You Need to Know

The picture graph on the next page shows how Jen used her money. The key shows that each picture stands for five dollars Jen spent.

❯ Practice the Skill

❶ How much did Jen spend on gifts?

❷ In what way did Jen use the most money?

❸ Did Jen spend more money on clothes or on books?

262

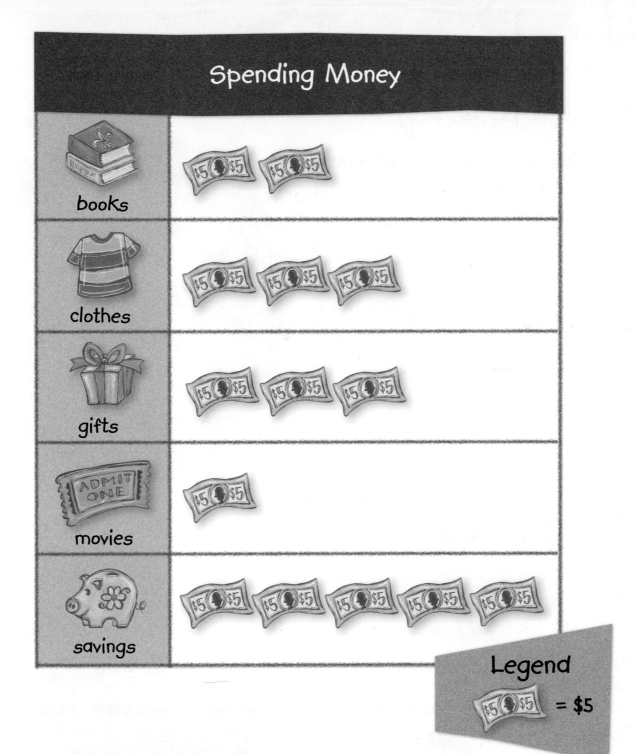

Spending Money

books	$5 $5
clothes	$5 $5 $5
gifts	$5 $5 $5
movies	$5
savings	$5 $5 $5 $5 $5

Legend

$5 = $5

❯ Apply What You Learned

Make It Relevant Make a picture graph to show how you would use $50.

History of Money

In the past, people would barter, or trade, for goods and services. They might trade eggs for cloth. Some people used beads, shells, or even salt as money. Today, people pay for goods and services with coins, paper money, checks, and credit cards.

salt

❶ Why do you think people started to use kinds of money?

seashells

amber

first coins, Turkey

264

2 These coins and bills were used long ago in the United States.

National Gold Bank notes

Continental U.S. bill, 1776

Gold coin, 1849

Gold-dust note

❸ Different kinds of money are used in other countries.

Chinese yuan

Indian rupees

Japanese yen

Canadian dollars

Mexican pesos

euros

Zimbabwean dollars

266

4 Bills and coins are not the only forms of money that people use.

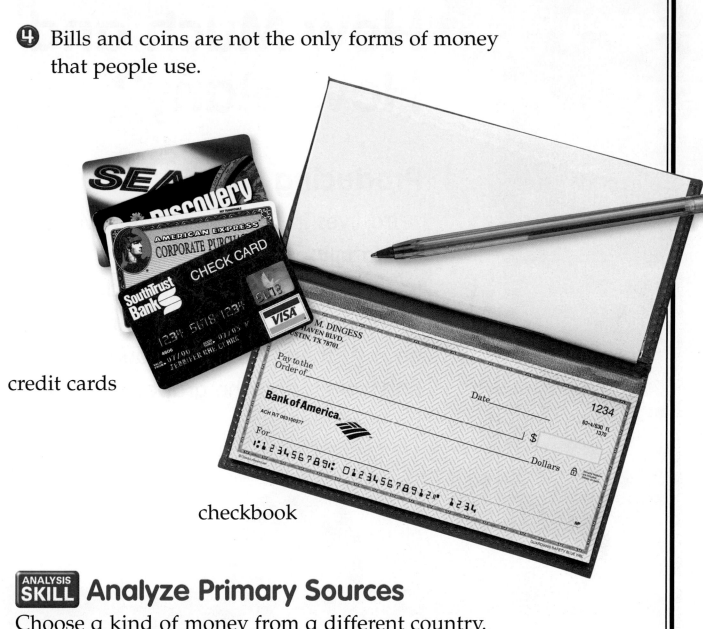

credit cards

checkbook

Analyze Primary Sources

Choose a kind of money from a different country. Find out about the people and things shown on the money. Why do you think they were chosen?

Visit PRIMARY SOURCES at www.harcourtschool.com/hss

How Much and How Many?

268

Producing Goods

Ira lives in the San Joaquin Valley. His family produces raisins for products such as raisin bread. To produce the raisins, the soil needs to be rich, there must be enough sun and water, and the grapevines must be healthy.

Raisins start as grapes. The grapes are left to dry in the sun.

Farmers who grow grapes for raisins can face problems. Without enough water, the grapes can burn up in the hot summer sun. Rain can ruin the raisins as they dry. Cold weather can freeze the grapes. If any of these events happen, raisins will be scarce. When something is **scarce**, there is not enough of it to meet everyone's wants.

(Reading Check) What problems do farmers face growing grapes for raisins?

drought

freeze

High and Low Prices

In the **marketplace**, the place where goods are sold, the price of goods can go up and down. If there are not many raisins to sell and many people want them and have the money to buy them, the price will go up. If there are many raisins to sell, or if not many people want them, the price will go down.

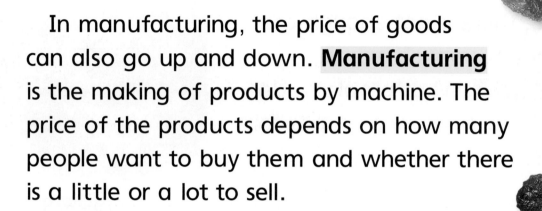

In manufacturing, the price of goods can also go up and down. **Manufacturing** is the making of products by machine. The price of the products depends on how many people want to buy them and whether there is a little or a lot to sell.

Sometimes goods are scarce because there are few raw materials to make them. Other times the raw materials cost too much. Goods can also be scarce if they take a long time to make. People have to pay more money to buy things that are scarce.

Reading Check Why might the price of something go up?

Summary When there is a lot of a product, people will pay less. When a product is scarce they will pay more.

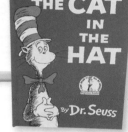

Review

1. 💡 Why do we make, sell, and buy more of some things than others?

2. **Vocabulary** What will happen to the cost of raisin bread if raisins are **scarce**?

3. ✏️ **Activity** Choose a raw material. Make a poster to show things that can be made from it.

4. (Focus Skill) **Categorize and Classify** Look around your classroom. Make a list of all the things that are made from the same raw material.

Make a Choice When Buying

❯ Why It Matters

When you go shopping, you may see many goods you want to buy. Some goods cost more money than you have. You must decide what you are willing to give up to get what you want.

❯ What You Need to Know

A **budget** is a plan that shows how much money you have and how much money you spend. To buy something that costs a lot, you can save money a little at a time.

You can put the money you save into a bank. A **bank** is a business that keeps money safe. Money in a bank earns more money. This extra money is called interest.

⟩ Practice the Skill

Imagine that you have earned ten dollars. You want to see a movie. You also want to buy new skates. You will have to make a choice about spending or saving your money.

● If you see the movie, what will you give up?

● If you decide to save for skates, what will you give up?

⟩ Apply What You Learned

Make It Relevant If you had ten dollars, would you spend the money right away or save it? Why?

Points of View

The Sidewalk Reporter asks:
"How do you make sure that you spend your money wisely?"

Carlos

"I put $25 in a jar to spend each week on extras."

Rick

"I'm saving for inline skates, so I don't spend a penny of what I earn."

View from the Past

Lewis and Clark: Bartering

From 1804 to 1806, Meriwether Lewis and William Clark explored the West. They took along goods to barter, or trade, with the American Indians for supplies.

Mrs. Walker

"I make a list of the things I want to buy to be sure they fit in my budget."

Mrs. Benitez

"When I see something I want to buy, I wait a week to make sure I really want it."

Mr. Johnson

"I use my money to pay my bills, and I save the rest."

ANALYSIS SKILL It's Your Turn

- Do you do any of the things that these citizens do? If so, which ones?
- How do you make sure that you spend your money wisely?

Lesson 4 Trading

What to Know
Why do countries trade goods with other countries?

- Groups and nations work together to trade goods they need.

- Groups and nations transport goods from one place to another.

Vocabulary
trade

 Focus Skill **Categorize and Classify**

California Standards
HSS 2.3.2

People in one country can't provide all the goods that its citizens want. They may not have all the raw materials to manufacture some goods. However, they may make other goods that people around the world want.

Banana plantation in Costa Rica

Working with Other Countries

People in one country trade with people in other countries to get raw materials or goods they do not have. **Trade** is the giving of one thing to get another. People in different countries may trade raw materials, goods, services, or money.

Reading Check Why do countries trade raw materials?

Geography

Trade with Other Countries

Two countries the United States trades with are Costa Rica and Ghana. We send both countries soybeans. Costa Rica sends us bananas. Ghana sends us cocoa that we use to make chocolate.

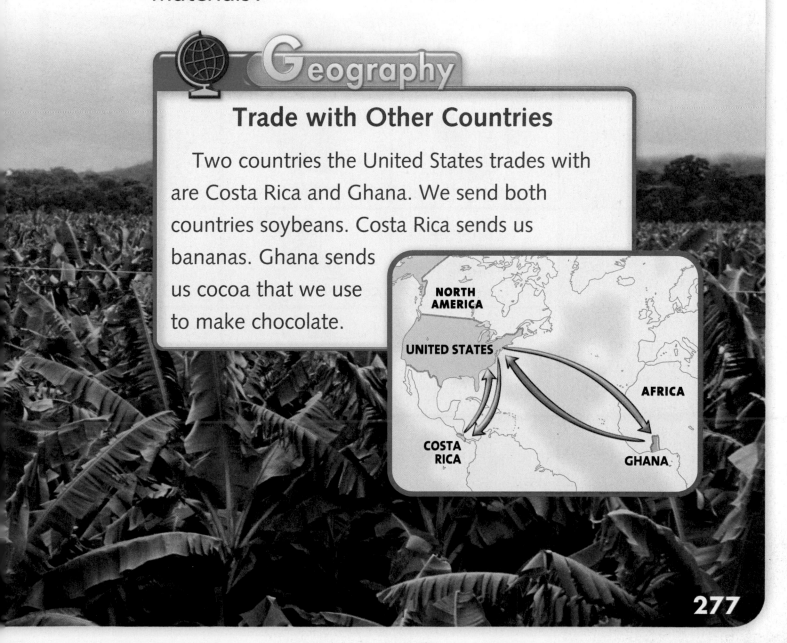

NORTH AMERICA

UNITED STATES

AFRICA

COSTA RICA

GHANA

Worldwide Trade

People in countries around the world sell raw materials to people in the United States who make goods. Then the United States sends the goods to other countries to be sold.

What product made in Germany might you buy?

Countries that Trade with the United States

Canada	lumber	maple syrup	newsprint
Mexico	fruits/vegetables	pottery	rugs
Japan	cameras	computers/games	CD players
Germany	clocks	tools	toys
China	furniture	silk cloth	tea

In just a few days, fresh fish from Canada can reach a table in the United States. In less than a week, carrots can come from Russia and be packed in your lunch. Oil from Venezuela provides fuel for trucks, trains, ships, and planes that take foods to markets.

Reading Check What are two countries where people trade with the United States?

Summary People in different countries trade with one another.

Review

1. 🔆 Why do countries trade goods with other countries?

2. **Vocabulary** What does the United States **trade** with Ghana?

3. 🖌 **Activity** Make labels for goods you want.

4. ⭐(Focus Skill) **Categorize and Classify** List the products that come from Canada.

279

All Work Together

by Woody Guthrie
illustrated by Melissa Iwai

My daddy said,
and my grandpaw, too,
there's a work-a work-a work-a
for me to do.
I can paint my fence
and mow my lawn.
But if we all work together,
well, it shouldn't take long.

We all work together with a
wiggle and a giggle.
We all work together with a
giggle and a grin.
We all work together with a
wiggle and a giggle.
We all work together with a
giggle and a grin.

My Momma told me
and my teacher told me, too,
there's all kinds of work
that I can do.
Dry my dishes,
sweep my floor.
But if we all work together,
it won't take so very long.

We all work together with a
wiggle and a giggle.
We all work together with a
giggle and a grin.
We all work together with a
wiggle and a giggle.
We all work together with a
giggle and a grin.

Response Corner

1 How does working together get
a job done more quickly?

2 **Make It Relevant** What work
do you do at home?

Port of Oakland

Get Ready

Every day, ships bring hundreds of brightly colored containers into the Port of Oakland. Inside the containers are goods such as car parts, furniture, food, and toys. Hundreds more containers leave the port on ships taking goods to other countries, such as China, Japan, Thailand, or Australia. Visitors to the port can see the trading of goods in action.

Locate It
California

Port of Oakland

What to See

Giant cranes take the containers off ships. Trucks, trains, and airplanes then move the containers to places all over the United States.

The Port of Oakland has rules that keep the land and water clean and healthy for plants and animals.

A Virtual Tour

GO ONLINE

Visit VIRTUAL TOURS at
www.harcourtschool.com/hss

Review

💡 **Work** Producers and consumers depend on each other for the goods and services they want. Producers provide the goods and services that consumers buy.

⭐ Focus Skill ## Categorize and Classify

Copy and fill in the chart to categorize and classify what you learned about the goods and services producers provide.

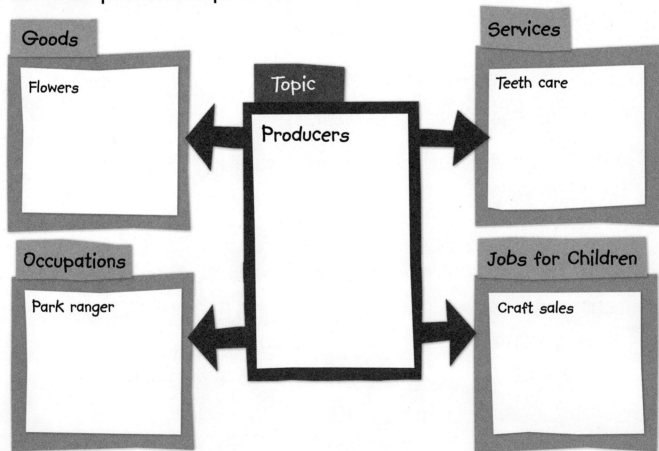

Goods
- Flowers

Services
- Teeth care

Topic
Producers

Occupations
- Park ranger

Jobs for Children
- Craft sales

Use Vocabulary

Match the word to its meaning.

1 things that can be bought and sold

2 work done for others

3 a place where goods are sold

4 a person who buys goods and services

5 a worker who grows, makes, or sells goods

producer
(p. 246)

goods
(p. 247)

services
(p. 247)

consumer
(p. 249)

marketplace
(p. 270)

Recall Facts

6 Why do people earn income?

7 What can make goods scarce?

8 Why do countries trade goods?

9 Which good can be made in a factory?

    A flowers   **C** oranges

    B raisins   **D** bicycle helmet

10 What do we call the work a person does to earn money?

    A occupation   **C** consumer

    B want   **D** free enterprise

Think Critically

11. **ANALYSIS SKILL** What would happen if the United States could not trade with other countries?

12. **Make It Relevant** How would your life be different if your family had to provide all of the goods it wanted?

Apply Chart and Graph Skills

13. What is the title of this bar graph?

14. How many bicycles were sold in Week 2?

15. Which week had the most sales?

16. Which week had the fewest sales?

Apply Chart and Graph Skills

Bakery Goods Sold on Thursday

Bread	$5	$5	$5	$5	$5
Muffins	$5	$5	$5	$5	
Cakes	$5	$5			
Bagels	$5	$5	$5	$5	

Legend

$5 = $5

17. What does this picture graph show?

18. Bakery customers spent the most money on which item?

19. How much money was spent on muffins?

20. Did Thursday's customers spend more on cakes or bagels?

Unit 5 Activities

Read More

A Family Music Shop
by Stephanie Buehler

Inside an Airplane Factory
by Sheila Sweeny

When Resources are Scarce
by Lisa deMauro

Show What You Know

Unit Writing Activity

Create a Sales Pitch Think of something to sell. Why would others want to buy it?

Write an Ad Write an ad to sell your item. Use details to describe the item.

Unit Project

Class Fair Plan a class fair.

- Provide goods or services.
- Create ads and flyers.
- Sell your goods or services at the class fair.
- Think about why some items sold better than others.

Visit ACTIVITIES at
www.harcourtschool.com/hss

People Make a Difference

Unit 6

2.5 Students understand the importance of individual action and character and explain how heroes from long ago and the recent past have made a difference in others' lives (e.g., from biographies of Abraham Lincoln, Louis Pasteur, Sitting Bull, George Washington Carver, Marie Curie, Albert Einstein, Golda Meir, Jackie Robinson, Sally Ride).

The Big Idea

People

Our lives are affected by the actions of heroes today and long ago.

What to Know

✓ Who are some scientists and inventors who have made a difference in people's lives?

✓ How have some heroes shown courage?

✓ What have people done to make life better for others?

✓ What heroes have helped the world by exploring new places and ideas?

Show What You Know

★ Unit 6 Test

✎ Writing: A Paragraph

🖌 Unit Project: A Hero's Day

People Make a Difference

6211

"Volunteers help organize the Special Olympics."

"Cheering helps the contestants keep going."

"I finished the race, and I feel proud."

Vocabulary

hero   A person who has done something brave or important.

(page 298)

courage   The ability to face danger bravely.

(page 308)

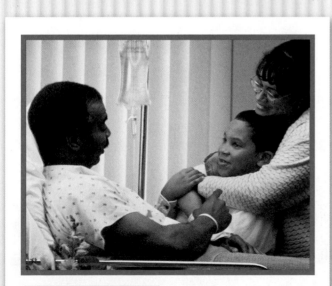

scientist   A person who studies and observes things in our world. (page 300)

explorer   A person who goes first to find out about a place. (page 322)

compassion   An understanding of how others feel and a wish to help them. (page 314)

GO ONLINE   INTERNET RESOURCES
Go to **www.harcourtschool.com/hss**
to view Internet resources for this unit.

Reading Social Studies

 **Recall and Retell**

As you read, be sure to recall and retell information. This will help you remember and understand what you read.

- To recall, think about what you have just read.

- To retell, put that information in your own words.

Practice the Skill

Read the following paragraph.

Recall   Susan B. Anthony was the first woman shown on United States money. She was honored this way because she spoke against unfair laws. In her lifetime, only men could vote. Her work helped change laws so that women could vote, too.

Apply What You Learned

Recall Detail

Susan B. Anthony was the first woman on American money.

Recall Detail

_____

_____

Recall Detail

_____

_____

Retell

_____

_____

_____

_____

_____

_____

Use this chart to write details you recall from what you just read. Then use your own words to retell what you read. Copy the chart and complete it.

Apply as You Read

As you read, recall and retell information about people in this unit.

Connect Ideas

When you read, you learn about many new ideas, facts, and events. Sometimes, one event leads to other events. By mapping how the events and ideas are connected, you will better understand what you read.

Practice the Skill

Lea mapped her ideas about the exploration of the West by Lewis and Clark. Copy Lea's chart. Think about these questions:

- Where did most people live at the time?

- What happened after they explored the West?

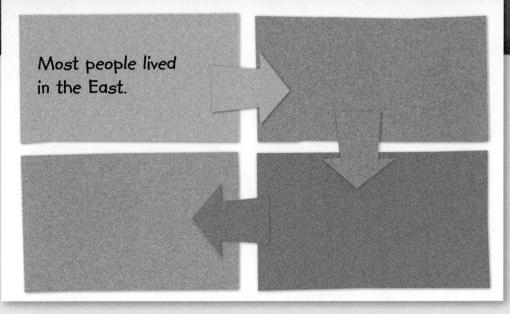

Most people lived in the East.

Read the paragraph below. Add your own ideas to the idea map.

In 1804, most people lived in the East. They did not know about the land west of the Mississippi River. Then Meriwether Lewis and William Clark were asked by the President to find out about the West. They explored the land and then shared what they found when they returned home. People could now make their homes in this new land.

Apply as You Read

In Unit 6, you will read how some people make a difference in the world. Map your ideas as you read. Show how one event leads to others.

A Tree for César Chávez

by Francisco X. Alarcón

illustrated by Maya Christina Gonzalez

an oak
we planted
on your day

an oak
in the middle
of the park

an oak
more bountiful
with time

an oak
with your features
and your spirit

296

an oak
with open
arms

an oak
for grown-ups
and children

an oak
ready to celebrate
your birthday

every March 31st
with tender leaves
of spring

Response Corner

What do you think the author means by using the words "an oak with your features and your spirit"?

297

Discovery and Invention

Heroes make a difference in people's lives with their words, actions, and discoveries. A **hero** is a person who has done something brave or important.

A Famous Inventor

As a child, Thomas Edison was curious. He asked many questions about how things worked. When he grew older, he wanted to find out how electricity could make tools and machines work.

What to Know
Who are some scientists and inventors who have made a difference in people's lives?

✔ Identify what makes a person a hero.

✔ Explain how inventors and scientists make a difference in people's lives.

Vocabulary
hero
invention
scientist

Focus Skill Recall and Retell

California Standards
HSS 2.5

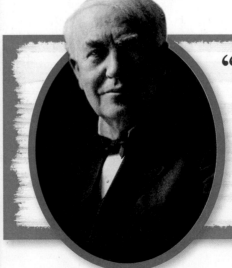

"Genius is one percent inspiration, ninety-nine percent perspiration."

Thomas Alva Edison

— from an article in <u>Harper's Magazine</u>, September, 1932.

During his life, Edison worked on more than one thousand inventions. An **invention** is a new product that has not been made before. Edison is most famous for inventing the electric lightbulb.

Reading Check What is one of Thomas Edison's inventions?

⚡**Fast Fact**

The night after Edison's funeral, Americans across the country dimmed their lights for one minute to show their respect.

The phonograph was another Edison invention. It could play recorded sounds.

Famous Scientists

Scientists observe things and make discoveries. Then they test their discoveries and work to make them safer and better.

The next time you drink a glass of milk, think about a scientist named Louis Pasteur. He found a way to kill harmful germs that get into milk and other foods.

"In the fields of observation chance favors only those minds which are prepared."

Louis Pasteur

—from a speech at University of Lille, Douai, France, December 7, 1854.

pasteurized milk

Think about George Washington Carver when you eat a peanut butter sandwich. Where Carver lived, the soil was poor from growing cotton for too long. Poor soil will not grow healthy plants.

George Washington Carver showed the farmers that growing peanuts, pecans, and sweet potatoes made the soil rich again. He found many ways to use these crops. Besides peanut butter, they could also be made into medicines, glue, and cereal.

Reading Check In what way were Louis Pasteur and George Washington Carver alike?

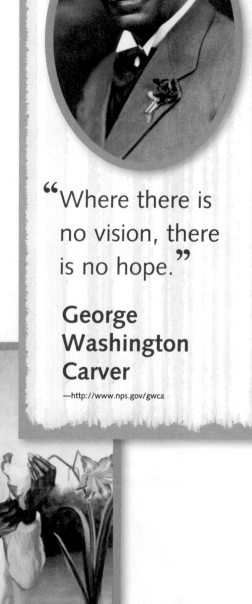

"Where there is no vision, there is no hope.**"**

George Washington Carver

—http://www.nps.gov/gwca

peanut plant

301

Prize-Winning Scientists

Each year, scientists from around the world can win an award called the Nobel Prize. The award honors scientists for the work that they do.

In 1903, Marie Curie was the first woman scientist to win a Nobel Prize. She discovered a metal that could be used to make X-ray pictures of bones.

"You cannot build a better world without improving the individuals."

Marie Curie

—from notes for book <u>Pierre Curie</u>, The MacMillan Company, 1923.

Nobel Prize

Albert Einstein won the Nobel Prize in 1921. He used math to explain ideas about time and space. He also studied the way light acts and moves.

Reading Check Why was the Nobel Prize given to Marie Curie and Albert Einstein?

Summary Inventors and scientists find ways to make a difference in people's lives.

" Anyone who has never made a mistake has never tried anything new. "

Albert Einstein

—from an article in <u>Saturday Evening Post</u>, October 26, 1929.

Review

1. Who are some scientists and inventors who have made a difference in people's lives?

2. **Vocabulary** Why are the people in this lesson **heroes**?

3. **Activity** Make a chart that lists the names of inventors and their inventions.

4. **Recall and Retell** Name a hero that you read about. Tell what he or she did to help others.

303

Read a Table

❱ Why It Matters

A **table** is a chart that organizes information. Knowing how to read a table can help you recall and retell information.

❱ What You Need to Know

The title tells you what the table shows. To read a table, put your finger on the first square of a row. Then read the information in that row. The column labels tell the kinds of information you.see.

❱ Practice the Skill

❶ What does this table show?

❷ Which inventors are listed in the table?

❸ Name one of Benjamin Franklin's inventions.

Inventors and Their Inventions

Inventors	Inventions or Improvements		
Benjamin Franklin	Franklin stove	lightning rod	bifocal glasses
Alexander G. Bell	telephone	hydrofoil	
Thomas Edison	talking doll	stock ticker	film projector
Garrett Morgan	gas mask	stop light	

◗ Apply What You Learned

Find out about another inventor and his or her inventions. How would you add the new information to this table?

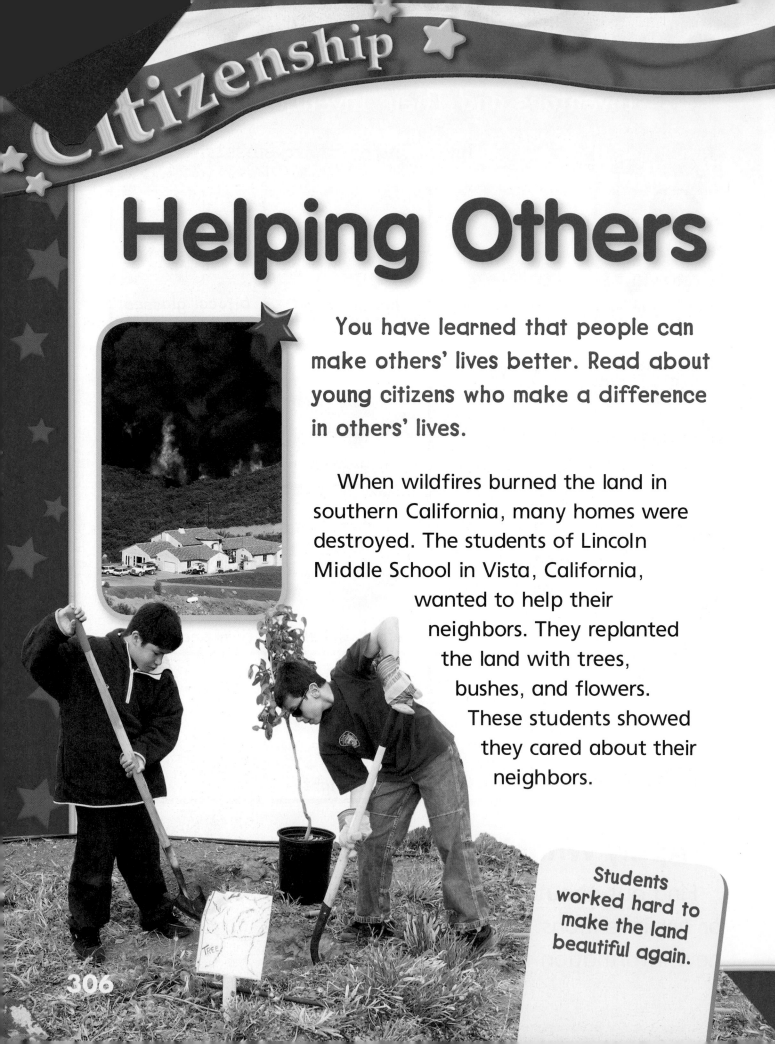

Helping Others

You have learned that people can make others' lives better. Read about young citizens who make a difference in others' lives.

When wildfires burned the land in southern California, many homes were destroyed. The students of Lincoln Middle School in Vista, California, wanted to help their neighbors. They replanted the land with trees, bushes, and flowers. These students showed they cared about their neighbors.

Students worked hard to make the land beautiful again.

Each year, millions of volunteers work on projects that help others. They might find food and clothing for people who do not have homes. Or they might collect books for school libraries. National Youth Service Day is an event that honors the ways volunteers help their communities.

Children choose different ways to help other people.

Did You Know?

Did you know that there are many groups that give children ideas for doing a community service? Find out about some of these groups:

★ Kids Care Clubs
★ America Youth Service
★ Youth Volunteer Corps of America

Think About It!

Make It Relevant What could you do to help your community?

Character and Courage

What to Know
How have some heroes shown courage?

✔ Explain why courage is important.

✔ Describe the actions of a hero who has made a difference in people's lives.

Vocabulary
courage

Focus Skill
Recall and Retell

California Standards
HSS 2.5

Heroes show courage. People who have **courage** face danger bravely. Heroes take action to stand up for what they believe.

Abraham Lincoln

Abraham Lincoln was our sixteenth President. Lincoln cared deeply for his country. He believed that slavery should end. Many people did not agree with him. Because of this, Americans fought against each other in the Civil War. Our country stayed strong because of Lincoln's leadership.

Reading Check What did Abraham Lincoln do for our country?

308

Sitting Bull

Sitting Bull was an American Indian leader. His people were the Sioux Indians who lived on the Great Plains. The United States government wanted the land where Sitting Bull and his people lived. It offered the Sioux new land and promised to keep settlers off it.

When that promise was broken, Sitting Bull led his people to fight for their land. Soldiers tried to arrest him. Sitting Bull died fighting for the rights of his people.

Reading Check What action did Sitting Bull take after the government broke its promise?

Dr. Martin Luther King, Jr.

In 1964, Dr. Martin Luther King, Jr., won the Nobel Peace Prize. Dr. King was a minister. He worked to find ways for people of all colors to live together in peace. His message was so important that Americans honor him with a holiday every January.

Reading Check What did Dr. King do to make a difference?

Jackie Robinson

Jackie Robinson dreamed of playing baseball. Many people did not want to let African Americans play. It took courage for Robinson to play anyway. Later, he helped other African Americans follow their dreams.

Reading Check How did Jackie Robinson show courage with his actions?

Summary Heroes show courage with their words and actions.

Review

1. How have some heroes shown courage?

2. **Vocabulary** Why is **courage** important?

3. **Write** Think about a hero who has shown courage. Write a letter to thank that person for taking action.

4. **Recall and Retell** How do Americans honor Dr. Martin Luther King, Jr.?

Tell Fact from Fiction

◗ Why It Matters

You need to be able to tell if what you read is true.

◗ What You Need to Know

1 A **fact** is a statement that can be proven true. **Nonfiction** books have only facts.

2 **Fiction** stories may seem real, but some of the information is made up.

3 A biography is a story about a person's life. It is nonfiction.

312

◗ Practice the Skill

Look at the two books. Decide which one is fact and which one is fiction.

◗ Apply What You Learned

Find a book in your library about a hero you would like to know more about. Will the book be fact or fiction?

✔ Identify ways people show compassion for others.

✔ Explain the importance of showing caring and compassion.

Vocabulary
compassion
volunteer

 Recall and Retell
Focus Skill

California Standards
HSS 2.5

Caring and Compassion

People who have **compassion** have an understanding of how others feel. They want to help others.

Dr. Antonia Novello

Dr. Antonia Novello was the Surgeon General of the United States from 1990 to 1993. The Surgeon General is a national spokesperson on health issues.

Showing Compassion

Dr. Novello was often ill as a child. Knowing what it was like to be a sick child gave her compassion for other sick children.

As Surgeon General, Dr. Novello spoke to children and teenagers about ways to stay healthy. She wanted to make sure that all children had the chance at a healthy life.

Reading Check What gave Dr. Antonia Novello compassion for sick children?

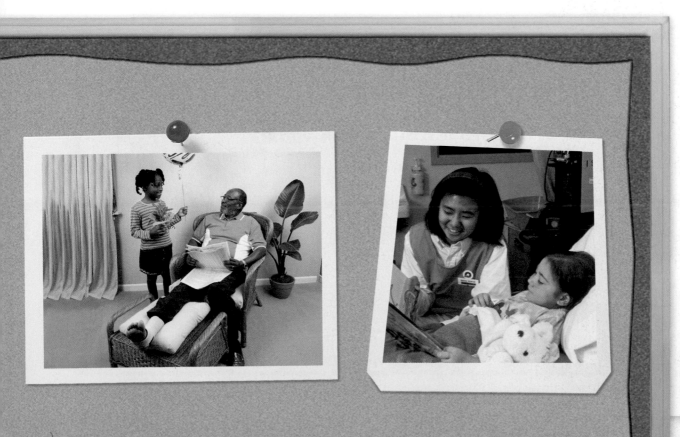

Mother Teresa

Mother Teresa was a nun, or church worker. She spent her life caring for poor people in India. First she worked as a teacher. Then she formed a group of nuns with a special goal.

These nuns wanted to help people who were unwanted, unloved, and uncared for. Mother Teresa and her helpers gave loving care, food, clothing, and shelter to anyone who needed their help.

Reading Check How did Mother Teresa show compassion for the poor people of India?

Children in History

Sadako Sasaki

In Japan, people say that if you fold 1,000 paper cranes you will get your wish. When Sadako Sasaki was 2 years old, a bomb fell on her city. By age 11, she had become very sick. Sadako started folding paper cranes, wishing to be healthy. When she knew that she would not get better, she changed her wish. Her new wish was for people to live in peace without bombs.

Caring for Others

" If you judge people, you have no time to love them. "

Mother Teresa

—http://www.quotedb.com

President Jimmy Carter

Jimmy Carter was the thirty-ninth President of the United States. After he left the White House, he wanted to keep helping people.

Jimmy Carter's wife, Rosalynn, joined him as a volunteer. A **volunteer** spends his or her free time making things better for people. The Carters work on a project called Habitat for Humanity. A habitat is a place to live, and humanity means "people." Habitat for Humanity volunteers build homes for people who don't have the money to buy one.

Reading Check What do Jimmy and Rosalynn Carter do to make life better for others?

Volunteers Help

Summary People care for others by showing compassion and working to make a difference in people's lives.

Review

1. 💡 What have people done to make life better for others?

2. **Vocabulary** How did Mother Teresa show **compassion** for people?

3. ✏️ **Write** Write a paragraph about something you could do to make a difference in someone's life.

4. (Focus Skill) **Recall and Retell** What do volunteers do?

Trustworthiness

Respect

Responsibility

Fairness

Caring

Patriotism

Why Character Counts

❖ How did Eleanor Roosevelt earn the nickname "First Lady of the World"?

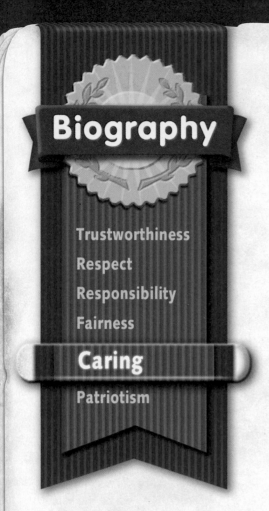

As wife of the President, Eleanor Roosevelt was First Lady for 12 years.

Eleanor Roosevelt

Eleanor Roosevelt was very shy as a child. Roosevelt's parents died when she was young, and her grandmother raised her. As a young woman, she volunteered to teach children who lived in poor neighborhoods. She saw how hard life was for the children's families. Roosevelt wanted to find ways to help them. She said, "The future belongs to those who believe in the beauty of their dreams."*

*http://womenshistory.about.com/
library/qu/blqurooe.htm

Eleanor Roosevelt with her husband and children in 1915

Roosevelt traveled the world as First Lady and became the "eyes and ears" of her husband, the President.

Bio Brief

1884　1962

When she became First Lady of the United States, Eleanor Roosevelt worked to get better living conditions for the poor. She also worked for equal rights for women and African Americans.

At the United Nations, Roosevelt helped write a bill of human rights for the people of the world. It says, "all human beings are born free and equal in dignity and rights."

Important Dates

1905 Marries Franklin Delano Roosevelt

1933 Becomes First Lady

1936 Begins writing her daily newspaper column, called "My Day"

1945–1951 Works as a delegate to the United Nations

GO ONLINE Interactive Multimedia Biographies
Visit MULTIMEDIA BIOGRAPHIES
at **www.harcourtschool.com/hss**

What to Know

What heroes have helped the world by exploring new places and ideas?

✔ Describe how explorers make a difference in people's lives.

✔ Explain how heroes have explored new places and ideas.

Vocabulary
explorer

Focus Skill Recall and Retell

California Standards
HSS 2.5

Exploring New Worlds

In class, we learned about **explorers**, people who go first to find out about something. That thing can be a place or an idea. We shared what we learned by imagining we were explorers.

Sally Ride

My name is Sally Ride. I was the first American woman to go into space.

In my two flights on the space shuttle, I did experiments. I studied space sickness, and I used a robot arm to pick up things outside the shuttle. Now I teach and write books about space for children.

Reading Check How was Sally Ride an explorer?

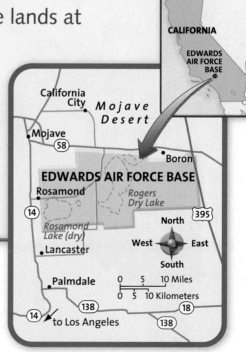

Geography

Edwards Air Force Base

Sometimes the weather is bad at the Kennedy Space Center in Florida. Then the shuttle lands at Edwards Air Force Base in California. The Air Force tests its planes there, too. The dried lakebeds of the Mojave Desert make a good place for planes to land. Pilots can see a long way there, too.

Golda Meir

I am Golda Meir. I was born in Russia, but I grew up in the United States. I believed that the Jewish people should have their own homeland. I worked to help start the country of Israel. In 1969, I became the first woman to be the leader of Israel.

Reading Check Why is Golda Meir a hero?

Charles Drew

I am Charles Drew. As a scientist, I studied blood. I found a way to keep blood so that it could be used later. The blood is kept in places called blood banks. Because of my discovery, people in hospitals can get blood when they need it.

Reading Check How does a blood bank help people?

Summary Some heroes explore new places or new ideas.

Review

1 What heroes have helped the world by exploring new places and ideas?

2 Vocabulary Why can Charles Drew be called an **explorer**?

3 Activity Find out about one of your heroes. Tell the class what he or she did to make a difference in people's lives.

4 **Recall and Retell** Who was the first American woman to go into space?

325

Someday I Will Read
by Pat Street
illustrated by Brenna Pierce

Narrator: The year is 1885 in Mayesville, South Carolina. Mary Jane McLeod is ten years old. She is African American.

African Americans in the South in 1885 do not have all the rights of white people. They cannot go to school. Mary Jane's mother works for a white family. Mary Jane helps her.

Scene I: *(Mama is folding clothes in the kitchen of a white family's home. Grace and Louise run in.)*

Grace: Come play with us, Mary Jane!

Mary Jane: May I, Mama?

Mama: Yes, but come back soon to help me. *(All the girls skip out the door.)*

Scene II: (*Playhouse with dolls and books*)

Mary Jane: What a nice playhouse!

Louise: Choose a doll. Let's have a tea party.

(*Mary Jane picks up a book. She looks inside it with wonder.*)

Grace: (*pointing*) Look, she has our book! Put that down, Mary Jane.

Louise: What would you do with a book, silly? You can't read! (*Grace and Louise laugh.*)

Mary Jane: (*proudly*) Someday I will read.

Scene III: *(Kitchen of Mary Jane's home)*

Mary Jane: There's a new school for African American children. May I go?

Mama: But it's a five-mile walk to town, child.

Papa: We need you here to help us pick cotton.

Mary Jane: Someone in this family needs to know how to read.

Mama: The child is right. She will make us proud.

Papa: All right, then, you may go to school.

Mary Jane: Thank you, thank you!

328

Scene IV: *(Kitchen of Mary Jane's home at night. She is reading by candlelight.)*

Narrator: Mary Jane never missed one day of school. She learned to read, and she became a teacher. Then she started her own school for African American girls. That school became a famous college.

All her life, Mary McLeod Bethune worked for fairness for African Americans. It all began the day she said, "Someday I will read."

Response Corner

❶ How did Mary McLeod Bethune make a difference in others' lives?

❷ **Make It Relevant** Why is reading important to you?

329

Mount Rushmore

Get Ready

A memorial helps people remember a person or an event. Many memorials honor United States Presidents. In South Dakota, the Mount Rushmore National Memorial honors George Washington, Thomas Jefferson, Theodore Roosevelt, and Abraham Lincoln.

Locate It
United States

South Dakota

What to See

The memorial honors Presidents from colonial times to the 1900s whose work was important to United States history.

George Washington

Thomas Jefferson

Theodore Roosevelt

Abraham Lincoln

In 1927, artist Gutzon Borglum planned the memorial at Mount Rushmore. The sculpture took more than 14 years to complete.

Borglum made plaster models of the Presidents' faces. He used information from paintings, photographs, and written descriptions.

Workers used drills and dynamite to carve the solid rock of the cliff. The faces on Mount Rushmore are 60 feet high!

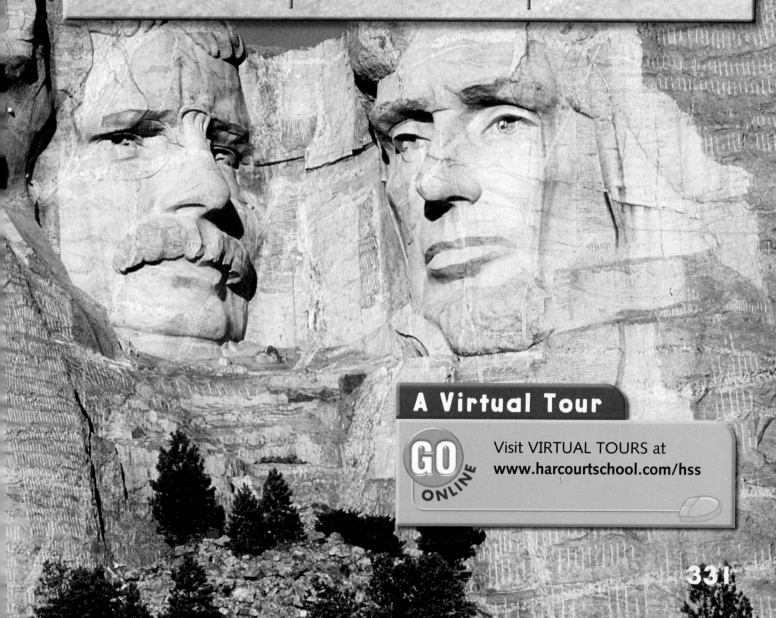

A Virtual Tour

GO ONLINE
Visit VIRTUAL TOURS at
www.harcourtschool.com/hss

💡 **People** Our lives are affected by the actions of heroes today and long ago.

⭐ Focus Skill **Recall and Retell**

Copy and fill in the chart to recall and retell what you have learned about heroes.

People Who Made a Difference

Recall Detail

Scientists observe things and make discoveries.

Recall Detail

_____

_____

Recall Detail

_____

_____

Retell

_____

_____

_____

_____

_____

Use Vocabulary

Choose the word that matches the description.

1 Marie Curie found a metal used for X-rays.

2 Sally Ride was the first American woman in space.

3 Jimmy Carter cares for others by building homes for people who do not have one.

4 Firefighters face danger bravely.

5 An explorer, a scientist, a leader, or a helper may be someone you know.

hero
(p. 298)

scientist
(p. 300)

courage
(p. 308)

compassion
(p. 314)

explorer
(p. 322)

Recall Facts

6 How did George Washington Carver help farmers?

7 In what ways was Golda Meir an explorer?

8 How did Dr. Martin Luther King, Jr., want to make a difference?

9 Who had new ideas about light and space?

    A Benjamin Franklin   **C** Albert Einstein

    B Mother Teresa   **D** Sally Ride

10 Who spends their free time helping others?

    A scientists   **C** explorers

    B farmers   **D** volunteers

Think Critically

11. **ANALYSIS SKILL** How would life be different today if Thomas Edison had not invented the electric lightbulb?

12. **Make It Relevant** How has showing courage made a difference in your life?

Apply Chart and Graph Skills

Discoveries That Changed Our Lives			
Medicine	Edward Jenner smallpox vaccine	Sir Alexander Fleming penicillin	Sir Frederick Grant Bunting insulin
Machines	James Watt steam engine	J. S. Thurman motorized vacuum cleaner	Mary Anderson windshield wipers
School Supplies	Helen A. Blanchard pencil sharpener	Edward Binney and Harold Smith crayons	George W. McGill stapler

13. What does this table show?

14. What did Helen A. Blanchard invent?

15. Who invented the vacuum cleaner?

16. Name three discoveries in medicine.

Apply Critical Thinking Skills

⑰ Which book do you think is fiction?

⑱ What clues lead you to believe it would be fiction?

⑲ What is the title of the biography?

⑳ Which book do you think would have more facts about Rosa Parks? Why?

Activities

Read More

Amelia Earhart
by Lisa Trumbauer

Paul Revere and Historic Boston
by Susan Ring

Martin Luther King, Jr.
by Jeri Cipriano

Unit Writing Activity

Choose a Hero Think of a hero in your life. Why is this person special?

Write a Paragraph Describe your hero in a paragraph. Tell how this person makes your life better.

Unit Project

Hero's Day Plan a day to honor heroes.

- Choose and research heroes.
- Gather costumes and props.
- Hold your Hero's Day with family members or other classes.

GO ONLINE Visit ACTIVITIES at
www.harcourtschool.com/hss

For Your Reference

ATLAS

RESEARCH HANDBOOK

BIOGRAPHICAL DICTIONARY

PICTURE GLOSSARY

INDEX

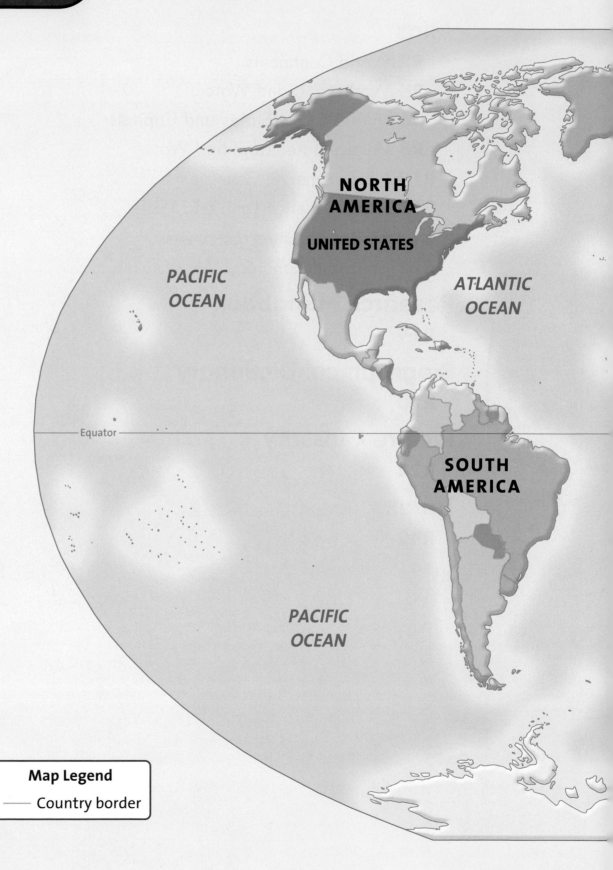

NORTH
AMERICA

UNITED STATES

PACIFIC
OCEAN

ATLANTIC
OCEAN

Equator

SOUTH
AMERICA

PACIFIC
OCEAN

Map Legend

— Country border

ARCTIC OCEAN

EUROPE

ASIA

PACIFIC OCEAN

AFRICA

INDIAN OCEAN

ATLANTIC OCEAN

AUSTRALIA

North
West   East
South

0   1,000   2,000 Miles
0   1,000   2,000 Kilometers

ANTARCTICA

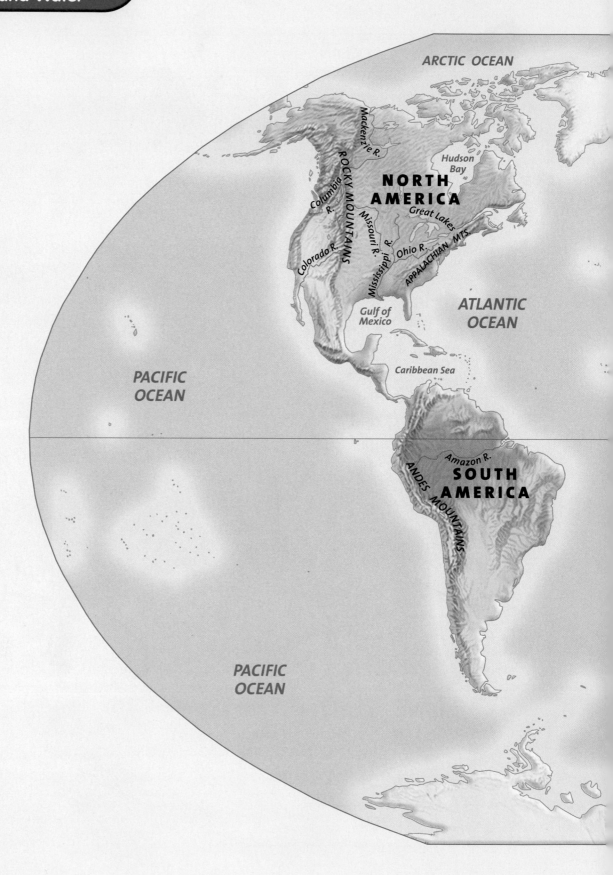

ARCTIC OCEAN

Mackenzie R.

Hudson
Bay

ROCKY MOUNTAINS

Columbia
R.

**NORTH
AMERICA**

Great Lakes

Missouri R.

Colorado R.

Ohio R.

Mississippi R.

APPALACHIAN MTS.

ATLANTIC
OCEAN

Gulf of
Mexico

PACIFIC
OCEAN

Caribbean Sea

Amazon R.

ANDES MOUNTAINS

**SOUTH
AMERICA**

PACIFIC
OCEAN

Greenland

ARCTIC OCEAN

URAL MTS.

Volga R.

EUROPE

ASIA

Black Sea

Caspian Sea

GOBI (DESERT)

Sea of Okhotsk

Mediterranean Sea

Atlas Mts.

HIMALAYAS

Huang He

Chang Jiang

PACIFIC OCEAN

SAHARA

Nile R.

Ganges R.

Arabian Sea

AFRICA

Bay of Bengal

South China Sea

Congo River

Lake Victoria

Lake Tanganyika

Sumatra

INDIAN OCEAN

New Guinea

Madagascar

Kalahari Desert

AUSTRALIA

GREAT VICTORIA DESERT

Darling R.

ATLANTIC OCEAN

Murray R.

North

West East

South

0   1,000   2,000 Miles

0   1,000   2,000 Kilometers

ANTARCTICA

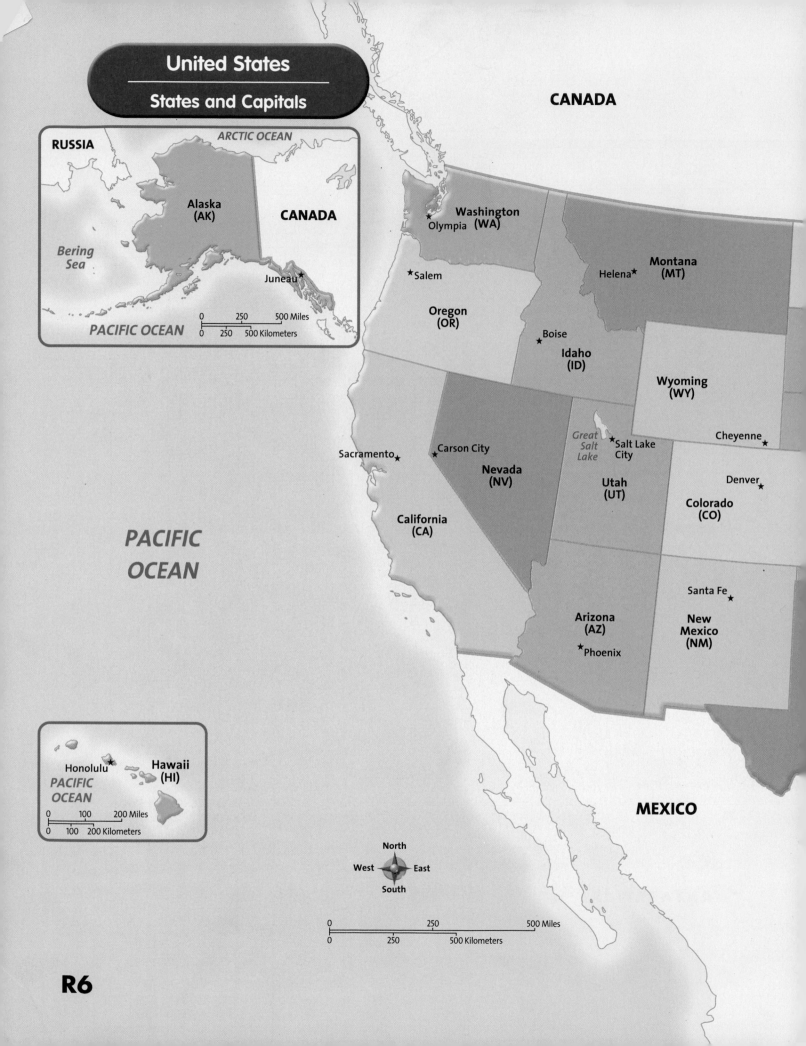

United States
States and Capitals

RUSSIA

ARCTIC OCEAN

Alaska
(AK)

CANADA

Bering Sea

Juneau ★

PACIFIC OCEAN

0   250   500 Miles
0   250   500 Kilometers

CANADA

★ Olympia   Washington (WA)

★ Salem

Helena ★   Montana (MT)

Oregon (OR)

Boise ★   Idaho (ID)

Wyoming (WY)

Great Salt Lake   ★ Salt Lake City

Cheyenne ★

Sacramento ★   ★ Carson City

Denver ★

Nevada (NV)

Utah (UT)

Colorado (CO)

PACIFIC

OCEAN

California (CA)

Santa Fe ★

Arizona (AZ)

New Mexico (NM)

★ Phoenix

Honolulu ★   Hawaii (HI)

PACIFIC OCEAN

0   100   200 Miles
0   100   200 Kilometers

MEXICO

North
West ← → East
South

0   250   500 Miles
0   250   500 Kilometers

R6

CANADA

North Dakota (ND)
★ Bismarck

Minnesota (MN)
St. Paul ★

Lake Superior

Lake Huron

Lake Michigan

(MI)
Lansing ★

Lake Ontario

Lake Erie

Maine (ME)
★ Augusta

Vermont (VT)
Montpelier ★

New Hampshire (NH)
★ Concord

New York (NY)
Albany ★

Boston ★

Massachusetts (MA)
Providence ★

Hartford ★ **Rhode Island (RI)**

Connecticut (CT)

Wisconsin (WI)
Madison ★

South Dakota (SD)
★ Pierre

Iowa (IA)
★ Des Moines

Nebraska (NE)
Lincoln ★

Illinois (IL)
★ Springfield

Indiana (IN)
★ Indianapolis

Ohio (OH)
Columbus ★

Pennsylvania (PA)
Harrisburg ★

Trenton ★

New Jersey (NJ)

Dover ★ **Delaware (DE)**

Kansas (KS)
Topeka ★

Missouri (MO)
Jefferson City ★

Kentucky (KY)
Frankfort ★

West Virginia (WV)
Charleston ★

Washington, D.C. ⊛

Annapolis ★

Maryland (MD)

Richmond ★ **Virginia (VA)**

Oklahoma (OK)
Oklahoma City ★

Arkansas (AR)
Little Rock ★

Tennessee (TN)
Nashville ★

Raleigh ★

North Carolina (NC)

Columbia ★

South Carolina (SC)

Atlanta ★

Mississippi (MS)
Jackson ★

Alabama (AL)
Montgomery ★

Georgia (GA)

Texas (TX)
Austin ★

Louisiana (LA)
Baton Rouge ★

Tallahassee ★

Florida (FL)

ATLANTIC OCEAN

BAHAMAS

Gulf of Mexico

CUBA

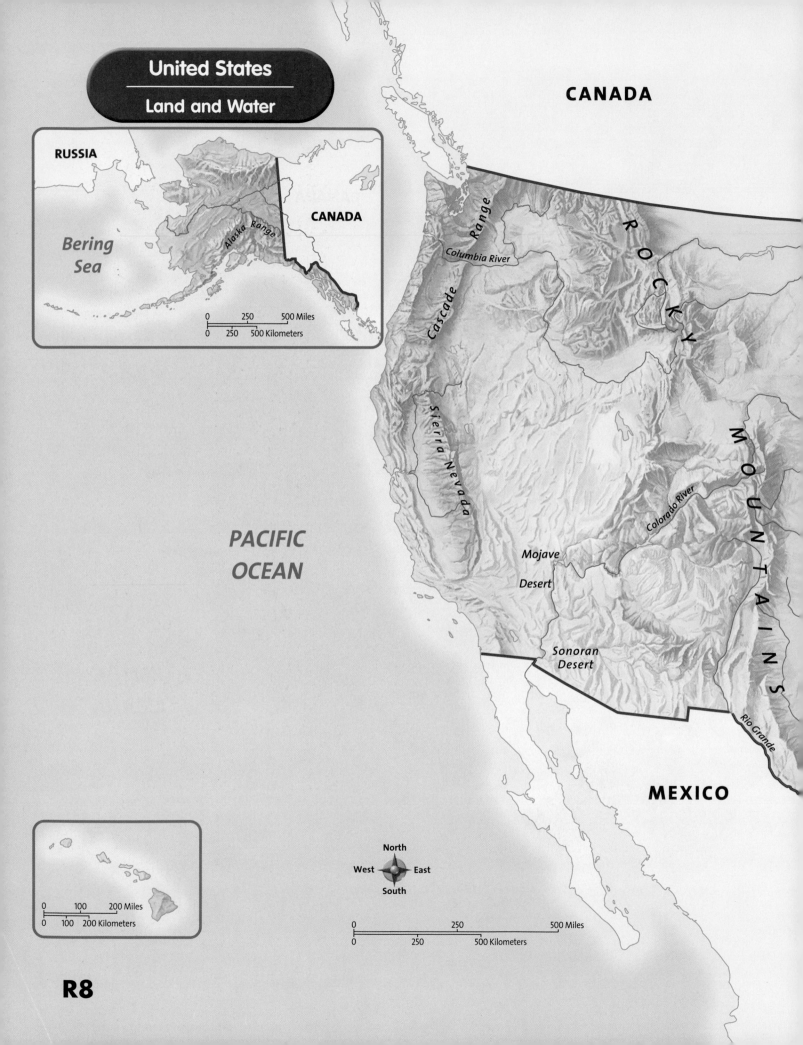

United States
Land and Water

RUSSIA

Bering Sea

Alaska Range

CANADA

0   250   500 Miles
0   250   500 Kilometers

CANADA

Cascade Range

Columbia River

R O C K Y

Sierra Nevada

M O U N T A I N S

Colorado River

Mojave Desert

PACIFIC OCEAN

Sonoran Desert

Rio Grande

MEXICO

North
West · East
South

0   250   500 Miles
0   250   500 Kilometers

0   100   200 Miles
0   100   200 Kilometers

CANADA

Lake Superior

Lake Huron

Lake Michigan

Lake Ontario

Lake Erie

G
R
E
A
T

P
L
A
I
N
S

Missouri River

Mississippi River

INTERIOR
PLAINS

Missouri River

Ohio River

Mississippi River

A
P
P
A
L
A
C
H
I
A
N

M
O
U
N
T
A
I
N
S

ATLANTIC
OCEAN

C
O
A
S
T
A
L

P
L
A
I
N

Rio Grande

Gulf of
Mexico

Straits of Florida

BAHAMAS

CUBA

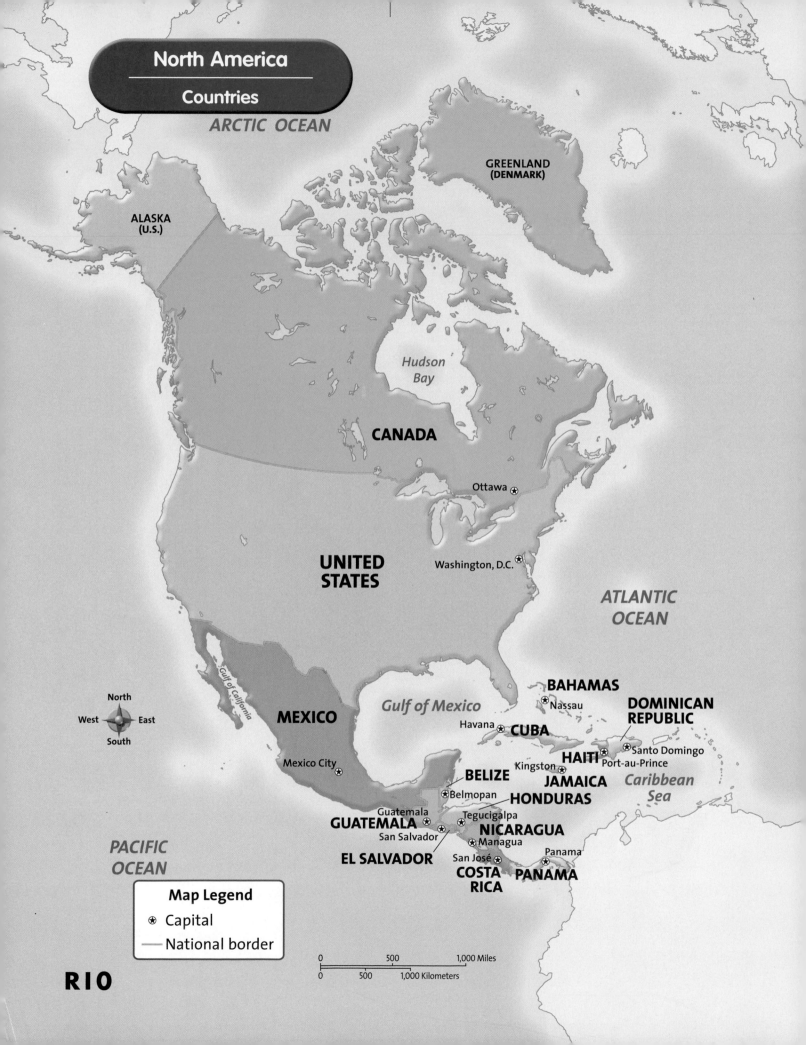

North America
Countries

ARCTIC OCEAN

GREENLAND
(DENMARK)

ALASKA
(U.S.)

Hudson
Bay

CANADA

Ottawa ✪

UNITED
STATES

Washington, D.C. ✪

ATLANTIC
OCEAN

BAHAMAS

✪ Nassau

DOMINICAN
REPUBLIC

Gulf of Mexico

Havana ✪ CUBA

Santo Domingo ✪

Gulf of California

MEXICO

HAITI

Port-au-Prince

Kingston

JAMAICA

Caribbean
Sea

Mexico City ✪

BELIZE

Belmopan ✪

HONDURAS

North

West ✪ East

Guatemala

Tegucigalpa

South

GUATEMALA ✪

NICARAGUA

San Salvador

Managua

PACIFIC
OCEAN

EL SALVADOR

San José

Panama

COSTA
RICA

PANAMA

Map Legend

✪ Capital

— National border

0   500   1,000 Miles

0   500   1,000 Kilometers

R10

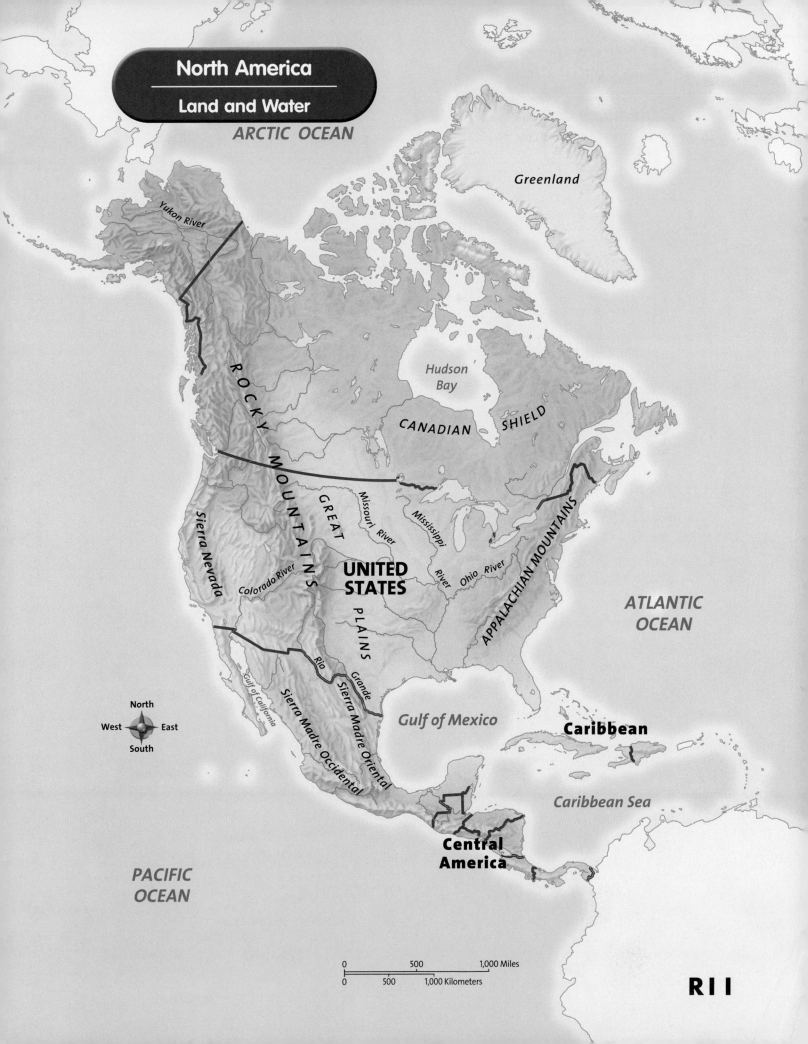

North America
Land and Water

ARCTIC OCEAN

Greenland

Yukon River

R O C K Y   M O U N T A I N S

Hudson Bay

CANADIAN   SHIELD

Missouri River

Mississippi River

Ohio River

Sierra Nevada

G R E A T

UNITED STATES

P L A I N S

APPALACHIAN MOUNTAINS

Colorado River

Gulf of California

Rio Grande

Sierra Madre Occidental

Sierra Madre Oriental

Gulf of Mexico

ATLANTIC OCEAN

Caribbean

Caribbean Sea

North
West — East
South

Central America

PACIFIC OCEAN

0	500	1,000 Miles
0	500	1,000 Kilometers

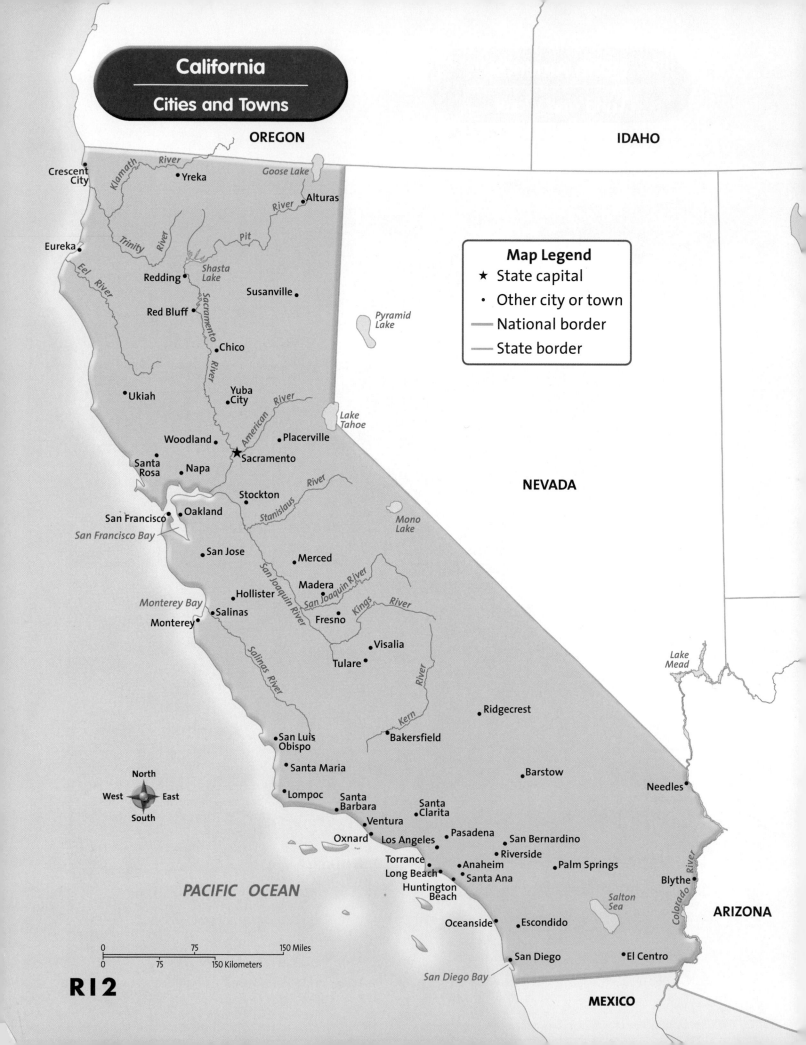

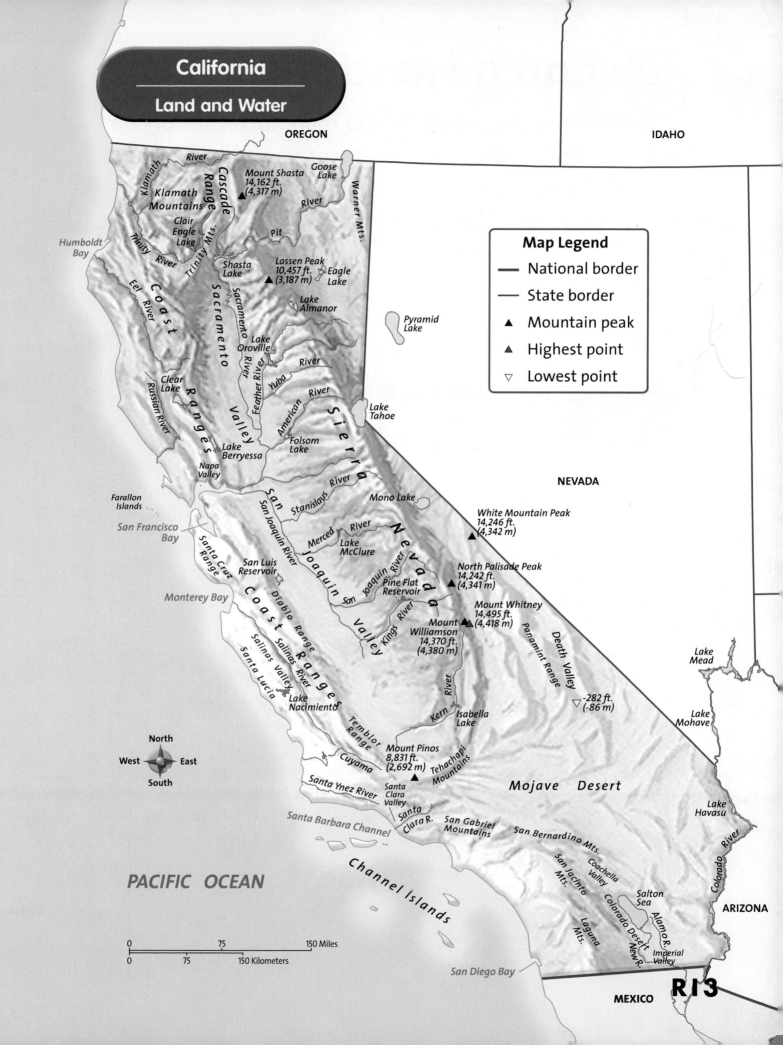

California
Land and Water

OREGON
IDAHO

Klamath River
Goose Lake
Mount Shasta 14,162 ft. (4,317 m)
Cascade Range
Klamath Mountains
Warner Mts.
River
Clair Engle Lake
Pit
Trinity Mts.
Humboldt Bay
Shasta Lake
Lassen Peak 10,457 ft. (3,187 m)
Eagle Lake
Trinity River
Lake Almanor
Sacramento River
Coast Ranges
Eel River
Sacramento Valley
Lake Oroville
Pyramid Lake

Map Legend
— National border
— State border
▲ Mountain peak
▲ Highest point
▽ Lowest point

Feather River
Yuba River
American River
Clear Lake
Russian River
Lake Berryessa
Folsom Lake
Lake Tahoe
Napa Valley
Sierra
NEVADA

Farallon Islands
San Francisco Bay
Stanislaus River
San Joaquin River
Mono Lake
White Mountain Peak 14,246 ft. (4,342 m)
Santa Cruz Range
Merced River
Lake McClure
Nevada
North Palisade Peak 14,242 ft. (4,341 m)
Monterey Bay
San Luis Reservoir
San Joaquin River
Pine Flat Reservoir
Mount Whitney 14,495 ft. (4,418 m)
Diablo Range
Coast Ranges
San Joaquin Valley
Kings River
Mount Williamson 14,370 ft. (4,380 m)
Panamint Range
Lake Mead
Santa Lucia
Salinas Valley
Salinas River
Lake Nacimiento
Temblor Range
Kern River
Isabella Lake
Death Valley
-282 ft. (-86 m)
Lake Mohave

North
West — East
South

Cuyama
Mount Pinos 8,831 ft. (2,692 m)
Tehachapi Mountains
Mojave Desert
Santa Ynez River
Santa Clara Valley
Santa Clara R.
Santa Barbara Channel
San Gabriel Mountains
San Bernardino Mts.
Coachella Valley
Lake Havasu

PACIFIC OCEAN
Channel Islands
San Jacinto Mts.
Colorado Desert
Salton Sea
Colorado River
ARIZONA
Laguna Mts.
Alamo R.
New R.
Imperial Valley

0   75   150 Miles
0   75   150 Kilometers

San Diego Bay

R13

MEXICO

Research Handbook

Sometimes you need to find more information on a topic. There are many resources you can use. You can find some information in your textbook. Other sources are technology resources, print resources, and community resources.

Technology Resources
- Internet
- Computer disk
- Television or radio

Print Resources
- Atlas
- Dictionary
- Encyclopedia
- Nonfiction book
- Magazine or newspaper

Community Resources
- Teacher
- Museum curator
- Community leader
- Older citizen

Technology Resources

The main technology resources you can use are the Internet and computer disks. Television or radio can also be good sources of information.

Using the Internet

Information on the Internet is always changing. Some websites have mistakes. Be sure to use a site you can trust.

> **Finding Information**

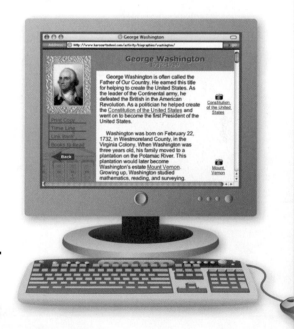

- Write down key words to look for. Make sure you spell words correctly.

- Use a mouse and a keyboard to search for information.

- With help from a teacher, parent, or older child, find the source you want to search.

- Type in your key words.

- Read carefully and take notes.

- If your computer is hooked to a printer, you can print out a paper copy.

Print Resources

Books in libraries are placed in a special order. Each book has a call number. The call number tells you where to look for the book.

Some books, such as encyclopedias and magazines and newspapers are kept together in a separate place. Librarians can help you find what you need.

❱ Atlas

An atlas is a book of maps. Some atlases show different places at different times.

❱ Dictionary

A dictionary gives the correct spelling of words. It tells you what words mean, or their definitions. It also gives the words' pronunciations, or how to say the words aloud. Words in a dictionary are listed in alphabetical order. Guide words at the top of the pages help you find your word.

dic•tion•ar•y [dik′ shən er′ e] n., pl. dic•tion•ar•ies A reference book that lists words in alphabetical order. It gives information about the words, including what they mean and how they are pronounced.

❱ Encyclopedia

An encyclopedia is a book or set of books that gives information about many different topics. The topics are listed in alphabetical order. An encyclopedia is a good place to start looking for information. You can also find encyclopedias on your computer.

❱ Nonfiction Books

A nonfiction book gives facts about real people, places, and things. Nonfiction books in the library are grouped by subject. Each subject has a different call number. Look in a card file or computer catalog to find a call number. You can look for titles, authors, or subjects.

❱ Magazines and Newspapers

Magazines and newspapers are printed by the day, week, or month. They are good sources of current information. Many libraries have a guide that lists articles by subject. Two guides are the <u>Children's Magazine Guide</u> and <u>Readers' Guide to Periodical Literature</u>.

Community Resources

Often, people in your community can tell you information you need. You can learn facts, opinions, or points of view by asking good questions. Before you talk to anyone, always ask a teacher or a parent for permission.

Listening to Find Information

❭ Before

- Think about what you need.
- Decide who to talk to.
- Make a list of useful questions.

❭ During

- Speak clearly and loudly.
- Listen carefully. You may think of other questions you want to ask.
- Be polite. Do not interrupt or argue.
- Take notes to help you remember ideas.
- Write down or tape record the person's exact words for quotes. Get their permission to use the quotes.
- Later, write a thank-you letter.

Writing to Get Information

You can also write to people in your community to gather information. You can write an e-mail or a letter. Keep these ideas in mind as you write:

- Write neatly or use a computer.

- Say who you are and why you are writing. Be clear about what you want to know.

- Carefully check your spelling and punctuation.

- If you are writing a letter, put in a self-addressed, stamped envelope for the person to send you a response.

- Thank the person.

Biographical Dictionary

The Biographical Dictionary lists many of the important people introduced in this book. Names are listed in alphabetical (ABC) order by last name. After each name are the birth and death dates. If the person is still alive, only the birth year is given. The page number tells where the main discussion of each person starts.

Adams, **Ansel** (1902–1984) American photographer. He is famous for his black-and-white photographs of the American wilderness. p. 70

Anthony, **Susan B.** (1820–1906) Women's rights leader. She helped get women the same rights that men have. p. 292

Anyokah Daughter of Sequoyah. At the age of six, she helped her father create a writing system for the Cherokee people. p. 166

Banneker, **Benjamin** (1731–1806) African American scientist and writer. He helped plan the streets of Washington, D.C. p. 98

Bell, **Alexander Graham** (1847–1922) American inventor. He invented the telephone. He also trained teachers to help people with hearing losses. p. 305

Carter, **Jimmy** (1924–) and **Rosalynn** (1927–) The 39th President and First Lady of the United States. Together, they work for peace and justice. p. 318

Carver, **George W.** (1864–1943) African American scientist. He worked on ways to improve farming in the South. p. 301

Chavez, **Cesar** (1927–1993) American farmworker. He worked to get fair treatment for all migrant workers. p. 213

Curie, **Marie** (1867–1934) French scientist. She was the first woman to win a Nobel Prize. p. 302

Drew, **Charles** (1904–1950) African American inventor. He invented the blood bank. p. 325

Edison, **Thomas** (1847–1931) American inventor. He invented the lightbulb and many other things. p. 298

Einstein, **Albert** (1879–1955) German scientist. He wrote about time, space, and energy. p. 303

Franklin, **Benjamin** (1706–1790) American leader, writer, and inventor. He helped write the Declaration of Independence. p. 305

Gutenberg, **Johannes** (c. 1400–1468) German metalworker and inventor. He invented the printing press and movable type. p. 54

Huerta, **Dolores** (1930–) Labor leader. She worked for the fair treatment of farmworkers. p. 220

King Abdullah II of Jordan (1962–) King of Jordan. He became king in 1999, following his father, King Hussein. p. 156

King, Dr. Martin Luther, Jr. (1929–1968) African American civil rights leader. He received a Nobel Prize for working to change unfair laws. p. 310

Kumaratunga, Chandrika (1945–) President of Sri Lanka. She is the first woman to serve as the country's president. p. 156

Lewis (1774–1809) and **Clark** (1770–1838) Leaders of an expedition to explore the American West. p. 274

Lincoln, Abraham (1809–1865) The 16th President of the United States. He was President during the U.S. Civil War and helped make it against the law to own slaves. p. 308

Marshall, Thurgood (1908–1993) First African American U.S. Supreme Court Justice. p. 152

Mbeki, Thabo (1942–) President of South Africa. p. 156

Meir, Golda (1898–1978) Prime Minister of Israel from 1969 to 1974. p. 324

Morgan, Garrett (1877–1963) African American business owner and inventor. He invented the traffic signal, the gas mask, and many other things. p. 305

Mother Teresa (1910–1997) Roman Catholic nun who spent most of her life helping poor people. She received a Nobel Peace Prize. p. 316

Novello, Dr. Antonia (1944–) First woman and first Hispanic to become the Surgeon General of the United States. p. 314

Pasteur, Louis (1822–1895) French scientist who discovered that germs spread diseases. His work saved many lives. p. 300

Ride, Sally (1951–) Astronaut and first American woman in space. p. 322

Robinson, Jackie (1919–1972) First African American to play modern major league baseball. p. 311

Roosevelt, Eleanor (1884–1962) First Lady of the United States for 12 years. She used her position to help people. p. 320

Schwarzenegger, Arnold (1947–) The 38th Governor of California. He was born in Austria and is an American actor, filmmaker, and politician. p. 140

Sitting Bull (1834?–1890) Sioux Indian leader. p. 309

Strauss, Levi (1829–1902) German American immigrant. He developed a successful business by selling goods to gold miners in California. p. 254

Tan, Amy (1952–) Asian American writer. Her stories about the Chinese culture are read all over the world. p. 34

Wright, Orville (1871–1948) and **Wilbur** (1867–1912) American flyers. They were the first to fly a motor-powered airplane. p. 312

Picture Glossary

The Picture Glossary has important words and their definitions. They are listed in alphabetical (ABC) order. The pictures help you understand the meanings of the words. The page number at the end tells where the word is first used.

ambassador
Someone who speaks for his or her government in another country. The **ambassador** from France met with the President. (page 162)

artifact

An object from the past. This **artifact** was found in Greece. (page 37)

ancestor
A family member who lived before you. My grandfather is my **ancestor**. (page 36)

ballot
A piece of paper that shows the choices for voting. The voter marked her choices on the **ballot**. (page 150)

bank

bank

A business that looks after people's money. People put money in the **bank** to keep it safe. (page 272)

budget

budget

A plan that shows how much money you have and how much money you spend. I make a **budget** every month. (page 272)

bar graph

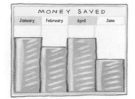

bar graph

A graph that uses bars to show how many or how much. This **bar graph** shows the money saved each month. (page 252)

business

business

The making or selling of goods or services. My parents have their own **business** selling flowers. (page 248)

border

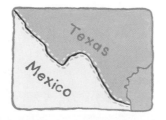

border

A line on a map that shows where a state or country ends. The red line shows the **border** between Texas and Mexico. (page 143)

calendar

calendar

A chart that keeps track of the days in a week, month, or year. A **calendar** shows that there are seven days in a week. (page 26)

capital

A city in which a state's or country's government meets and works. Washington, D.C., is the **capital** of the United States. (page 143)

citizen

A person who lives in and belongs to a community. Nick is a **citizen** of the United States. (page 132)

cardinal directions

The main directions of north, south, east, and west. The **cardinal directions** help you find places on a map. (page 96)

city

A very large town. There are many tall buildings in my **city**. (page 82)

change

Something that makes a thing become different. In fall, a **change** happens to the color of some leaves. (page 23)

climate

The kind of weather a place has over a long time. The rain forest has a very wet **climate**. (page 194)

communication

The sharing of ideas and information. The firefighter uses a radio for **communication** with other firefighters. (page 52)

Congress

The group of citizens chosen to make decisions for the country. **Congress** votes on new laws. (page 146)

community

A group of people who live or work together. It is also the place where they live. My family has lived in our **community** for many years. (page 24)

consequence

Something that happens because of what a person does. The **consequence** of wearing muddy shoes is a dirty floor. (page 137)

compassion

An understanding of how others feel. My mom has **compassion** for me when I get hurt. (page 314)

conservation

Working to save resources or to make them last longer. **Conservation** of electricity is a good idea. (page 192)

Constitution

The plan of government for the United States. The **Constitution** says that every adult citizen has the right to vote. (page 148)

cooperate

To work together. My family likes to **cooperate** on projects. (page 164)

consumer

A person who buys and uses goods and services. This **consumer** is buying food for a picnic. (page 249)

council

A group of citizens chosen to make decisions for all the people. The **council** is discussing where to build the playground. (page 138)

continent

One of the seven main land areas on Earth. We live on the **continent** of North America. (page 111)

country

An area of land with its own people and laws. We are proud of our **country**, the United States. (page 90)

courage

The ability to face danger bravely. The firefighter had the **courage** to put out the fire. (page 308)

crop

A plant that people grow for food or other needs. Corn is an important **crop** in the United States. (page 194)

culture

A group's way of life. Music and dance are parts of my **culture**. (page 131)

diagram

A picture that shows the parts of something. The **diagram** helped me put my toy together. (page 42)

directional indicator

The symbol on a map that shows directions. The **directional indicator** shows directions. (page 96)

distributor

A person who brings a product from the processing plant to the market. The **distributor** drove the orange juice to the market. (page 216)

election

A time when people vote for their leaders. The **election** to choose the President is held in November. (page 147)

event

Something that happened. A birthday party is a happy **event**. (page 28)

embassy

A building in which an ambassador lives. The ambassador lives in the **embassy**. (page 162)

explorer

A person who goes first to find out about a place. Lewis and Clark were famous **explorers**. (page 322)

equator

An imaginary line that divides Earth into northern and southern halves. Most of South America is south of the **equator**. (page 96)

F

fact

A piece of information that is true. It is a **fact** that humans have walked on the moon. (page 312)

factory

A building in which people use machines to make goods. The car was made in a **factory** in Detroit. (page 250)

freedom

The right of people to make their own choices. Americans have the **freedom** to vote. (page 132)

fiction

Stories that may seem real, but in which some of the information is made up. The story of Little Red Riding Hood is **fiction**. (page 312)

free enterprise

The freedom to start and run any kind of business. **Free enterprise** helps these children earn money. (page 258)

flowchart

A chart that shows the steps needed to make or do something. The **flowchart** shows how to make a picture frame. (page 218)

fuel

A resource, such as oil, that can be burned for heat or energy. Gasoline is a **fuel** used in cars. (page 191)

geography

The study of Earth and its people. **Geography** teaches us about Earth and the people on it. (page 18)

government

The group of citizens that runs a community, state, or country. Our **government** needs strong leaders. (page 136)

globe

A model of Earth. We can find countries on our classroom **globe**. (page 110)

governor

The leader of a state's government. Every state has a **governor**. (page 140)

goods

Things that can be bought and sold. This store sells many kinds of **goods**. (page 247)

heritage

Something that is handed down from ancestors. My grandmother teaches me about my **heritage**. (page 38)

hero

A person who has done something brave or important. This **hero** saved someone's life. (page 298)

income

The money people earn for the work they do. Miguel will use his **income** to buy lemonade. (page 256)

history

The study of things that happened in the past. The **history** of our country is interesting. (page 22)

invention

A new product that has not been made before. The lightbulb was an **invention** of Thomas Edison. (page 299)

 I

immigrant

A person who comes from somewhere else to live in a country. My great-grandfather was an Irish **immigrant**. (page 103)

 J

judge

The leader of a court. The **judge** punished the lawbreaker. (page 139)

landform

A kind of land with a special shape, such as a mountain, hill, or plain. A mountain is a large **landform**. (page 92)

location

The place where something is. The map will help you find your **location**. (page 76)

law

A rule that people in a community must follow. A speed limit **law** keeps people safe. (page 136)

M

majority rule

Rule by more than half of the people in a community. The decision to build a new school was made by **majority rule**. (page 150)

legislature

A group of citizens chosen to make decisions for a state. The **legislature** will decide where to build a new road. (page 140)

manufacturing

The making of products by machine. Robots are used in the **manufacturing** of car parts. (page 270)

map

A drawing that shows where places are. Can you find an island on this **map**? (page 111)

map scale

The part of a map that helps you find distance. The **map scale** can help you find out how far it is from Charleston to Elkins. (page 88)

map grid

A set of lines that divide a map into columns and rows of squares. The star is at square C-3 on the **map grid**. (page 80)

map symbol

A small picture or shape on a map that stands for a real thing. This **map symbol** stands for a mountain. (page 113)

map legend

The part of a map that shows what the symbols mean. Look for the symbol of the bridge in the **map legend**. (page 77)

map title

The title of a map. The **map title** tells what the map shows. (page 77)

market

The place where people buy and sell goods. The **market** sells many fruits and vegetables. (page 212)

nation

A country. Russia is a **nation**. (page 155)

marketplace

Where people buy and sell goods and services. A lot of things are sold at the **marketplace**. (page 270)

natural resource

Something found in nature that people can use. Oil is a **natural resource**. (page 188)

mayor

The leader of a city or town government. The **mayor** makes important decisions for our community. (page 138)

Daily News
Schwarzenegger WINS Election

nonfiction

Stories that contain only facts. Newspaper stories are **nonfiction**. (page 312)

O

occupation

The work a person does to earn money. My dad's **occupation** is being a doctor. (page 256)

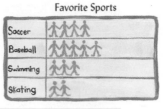

picture graph

A graph that uses pictures to stand for numbers of things. The **picture graph** shows that people chose baseball the most. (page 262)

ocean

A very large body of salty water. Ships sail across the **ocean**. (page 111)

pioneer

A person who is one of the first to live in a new land. Many **pioneers** traveled west in covered wagons. (page 100)

P

past

The time before now. George Washington lived in the **past**. (page 22)

present

Right now. Today is the **present**. (page 24)

President

The leader of the United States government. George Washington was the first **President** of the United States. (page 147)

producer

A person who makes, grows, or sells goods. This **producer** grows fruit to sell. (page 246)

problem

Something difficult or hard to understand. The **problem** with the pipe is that it leaks. (page 164)

product

Something that is made by nature or by people. Applesauce is a **product** made from apples. (page 208)

processing plant

A place where food is turned into food products. Peanuts are made into peanut butter at a **processing plant**. (page 214)

product map

A map that shows where products are found or made. This **product map** shows where corn is grown. (page 208)

R

raw material

A resource used to make a product. Wood is a **raw material** used to make furniture. (page 212)

route

A way to go from one place to another. The **route** on this map is easy to follow. (page 106)

responsibility

Something that a citizen should take care of or do. It is my **responsibility** to take these glasses I found to the store owner. (page 134)

rural

An area in the country, far from a city. This **rural** area is very peaceful. (page 84)

rights

Freedoms. Freedom of speech is one of our many **rights**. (page 132)

S

scarce

Hard to find because there is not much of it. When money is **scarce**, George cannot buy candy. (page 269)

scientist

A person who observes things and makes discoveries. Albert Einstein was a **scientist**. (page 300)

source

The place something comes from. An encyclopedia is a good **source** of information. (page 37)

services

Work done for others. We paid the waiter for his **services**. (page 247)

state

A part of a country. California is one of our fifty **states**. (page 82)

solution

The way people agree to solve a problem. The **solution** to the leaky pipe is to replace it. (page 164)

storyboard

A board that uses words and pictures to show events in order. A **storyboard** helps tell what happened. (page 28)

suburb

A community near a large city. This **suburb** is about thirty miles from the city. (page 83)

tax

Money paid to the government and used to pay for services. The **tax** we pay at the store helps pay for building roads. (page 146)

Supreme Court

The highest court in the United States. The **Supreme Court** decides the most important cases. (page 148)

technology

The use of new inventions in everyday life. Computers are a useful **technology**. (page 202)

table

A chart that shows information in rows and columns. A **table** can be used to compare things. (page 304)

time line

A line that tells when things happened. This **time line** shows holidays. (page 32)

trade

The exchange of one thing for another. Is this a fair **trade**? (page 277)

treaty

A contract or agreement. The two countries signed a **treaty**. (page 162)

tradition

Something that is passed on from older family members to children. Wearing kilts is a Scottish **tradition**. (page 51)

U

urban

In, of, or like a city. They live in an **urban** area. (page 82)

transportation

The moving of goods and people from place to place. Buses and airplanes are both used for **transportation**. (page 49)

V

volunteer

A person who works without being paid. I am a **volunteer** for my favorite charity. (page 318)

vote

A choice that gets counted. The person who gets the most **votes** is the winner. (page 150)

want

Something that people would like to have but do not need. I have more **wants** than I can afford. (page 260)

Index

The index tells where information about people, places, and events in this book can be found. The entries are listed in alphabetical order. Each entry tells the page or pages where you can find the topic.

INDEX

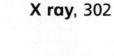

For permission to reprint copyrighted material, grateful acknowledgment is made to the following sources:

Aladdin Paperbacks, an imprint of Simon & Schuster Children's Publishing Division: From *The Story of Johnny Appleseed* by Aliki. Copyright © 1963 by Aliki Brandenberg.

Children's Book Press, San Francisco, CA: "A Tree for César Chávez" from *Laughing Tomatoes and Other Spring Poems* by Francisco Alarcón, illustrated by Maya Christina Gonzalez. Text copyright © 1997 by Francisco Alarcón; illustrations copyright © 1997 by Maya Christina Gonzalez. "My Grandma's Stories"/"Los cuentos de mi abuelita" from *A Movie in My Pillow/ Una película en mi almohada* by Jorge Argueta. Text copyright © 2001 by Jorge Argueta.

Clarion Books/Houghton Mifflin Company: From *To Fly: The Story of the Wright Brothers* by Wendie C. Old, illustrated by Robert Andrew Parker. Text copyright © 2002 by Wendie C. Old; illustrations copyright © 2002 by Robert Andrew Parker.

Cobblestone Publishing, Inc., 30 Grove Street, Suite C, Peterborough, NH 03458: From "Hail to the Chief" by John P. Riley in *Appleseeds: American Presidents,* April 2004. Text copyright © 2004 by Carus Publishing Company.

Folkways Music Publishers, Inc., New York, NY: Lyrics from "All Work Together" by Woody Guthrie. TRO – © copyright 1956 (renewed) and 1963 (renewed) by Folkways Music Publishers, Inc. Published by Folkways Music Publishers, Inc.

Harcourt, Inc.: The *Tortilla Factory* by Gary Paulsen, illustrated by Ruth Wright Paulsen. Text copyright © 1995 by Gary Paulsen; illustrations copyright © 1995 by Ruth Wright Paulsen.

Holiday House, Inc.: From *Supermarket* by Kathleen Krull, illustrated by Melanie Hope Greenberg. Text copyright © 2001 by Kathleen Krull; illustrations copyright © 2001 by Melanie Hope Greenberg.

Henry Holt and Company, LLC: From *Wee and the Wright Brothers* by Timothy R. Gaffney, illustrated by Bernadette Pons. Text copyright © 2004 by Timothy R. Gaffney; illustrations copyright © 2004 by Bernadette Pons.

Barbara S. Kouts, on behalf of Joseph Bruchac: "How the Prairie Became Ocean" from *Four Ancestors: Stories, Songs, and Poems from Native North America* by Joseph Bruchac. Text copyright © 1996 by Joseph Bruchac.

G. P. Putnam's Sons, A Division of Penguin Young Readers Group, A Member of Penguin Group (USA) Inc., 345 Hudson St., New York, NY 10014: Covered Wagons, Bumpy Trails by Verla Kay, illustrated by S. D. Schindler. Text copyright © 2000 by Verla Kay; illustrations copyright © 2000 by S. D. Schindler.

Random House Children's Books, a division of Random House, Inc.: Cover illustration from *The Cat in the Hat* by Dr. Seuss. TM & copyright © 1957, renewed 1985 by Dr. Seuss Enterprises, L.P.

The Watts Publishing Group Limited, 96 Leonard Street, London EC2A 4XD: When I Was Young by James Dunbar, illustrated by Martin Remphry. Text copyright © 1998 by James Dunbar; illustrations copyright © 1998 by Martin Remphry. Originally published in the UK by Franklin Watts, a division of The Watts Publishing Group Limited, 1999.

PHOTO CREDITS

PLACEMENT KEY: (t) top; (b) bottom; (l) left; (r) right; (c) center; (bg) background; (fg) foreground; (i) inset.

COVER: (t) Ron Stroud/Masterfile; (bg) Allen Birnbach/Masterfile.

FRONTMATTER: blind iiv (b) David Lawrence/Panoramic Images; v (b) Security Pacific Collection/Los Angeles Public Library; (br) Anaheim Public Library; (fg) Lawrence Migdale, vi (b) Lester Lefkowitz/ Corbis; vii (b) Joseph Sohm/Chromo Sohm/ Corbis; viii (b) Dave G. Houser/Corbis; (fg) Ken James/Corbis; ix (fg) Getty Images; x (bg) Monsoon Images/PictureQuest; xii (bg) Coco McCoy/Rainbow; xiv (b) Jonathan Nourok/Photo Edit; xv (b) Paul A. Souders/Corbis; I2 (t) C.E. Watkins/Corbis; (b) Enzio Petersen/Bettmann/Corbis; I3 (c) Stephanie Maze/Corbis; I8 (b) Zandria Muench Beraldo/Corbis; (c) Getty Images; I9 (t) Greg Cranna/Index Stock Imagery; (c) Getty Images; (b) Greg Probst/Corbis; I12 (b) Richard Hamilton Smith Photography; I13 (b) Stone; Getty Images.

UNIT 1: 1 (tl), (tr), (c), (cl) Anaheim Public Library; (c) Walter & Zuelma Goodall; (cr) Taxi/Getty Images; (br) Lawrence Migdale; 2 (t) Eastman's Originals Collection/ Department of Special Collections/ General Library/ University of California/ Davis; (br) David Young-Wolff/PhotoEdit; 3 (t) David Barker/ Ohio Historical Society; (cr) Betts Anderson Loman/PhotoEdit; (bl) Rick Gomez/Masterfile; (br) Anaheim Public Library; 4 (b) Inga Spence/Index Stock Imagery; 7 (c) Picture History/ LLC; 22 (bg) Rob Lewine/Corbis; 23 (t) Taxi/ Getty Images; (c) Bill Aron/PhotoEdit; (b) Security Pacific Collection / Los Angeles Public Library; 24 (c) City of Santa Ana Local History Room; (b) Tony Freeman/ PhotoEdit; 25 (l) Robert W. Ginn/PhotoEdit; (r) Tom Paiva Photography; 28 (c) Comstock Images; (b) Stone/Getty Images; 29 (bl) Stone/Getty Images; 30 (b) Rob Crandall/ Stock Connection/PictureQuest; 31 (t) Owen Franken/Stock/ Boston; 32 (bl), (br) Eric & Nathalie Cumbie; 34 (b) Lawrence Lucier/Getty Images; 35 (tl) Jim McHugh Photography; (c) Ms. Amy Tan; 36 (c) DigitalVision/PictureQuest; 39 (br) DigitalVision/PictureQuest; 40 (c), (cr) James Huy Vu/ Union of Vietnamese Student Association; (bl) Photodisc Green/ Getty Images; 41 (c) Jacques Pavlovsky/

Corbis; 44 (bl) Spencer Grant/PhotoEdit; (br) Spencer Grant; Photo Edit; 45 (tr) Vince Streano/Corbis; (c) www.californiabell. com; (br) California State University/ Fresno; 46 (t) David Barker/ Ohio Historical Society; (cr) Corbis; (b) San Francisco Cable Car Museum; 47 (t) Shades of L.A. Archives / Los Angeles Public Library; (c) David Young-Wolff/PhotoEdit; (inset) Paul Thompson/Index Stock Imagery; 48 (b) Ed Young/Corbis; 49 (fg) Aneal Vohra/Index Stock Imagery; (bg) Medioimages/Inmagine; 51 (tr) George Shelley/Corbis; (cr) Eduardo Ripoll/Age Fotostock America; (br) Ariel Skelley/Corbis; (fg) Paul Barton/Corbis; 52 (c) Joe Carini/Index Stock Imagery; 53 (t) Corbis; (cl), (cl) Photodisc Green/Corbis; 54 (c) Kaz Chiba/Getty Images; (cr) Tom Grill/Corbis; 55 (cl) Stone+/Getty Images; (c) Franco Vogt/Corbis; (cr) Chuck Savage/ Corbis; (b) Bettmann/Corbis; 58 (b) Michael Newman/PhotoEdit; 59 (tl) Los Angeles Public Library/ Security Pacific Collection; (tr), (c), (bl) Montes De Oca; (br) Michael Newman/PhotoEdit.

UNIT 2: 65 (b) Lawrence Migdale; (bg) Bob and Suzanne Clemenz/AGPix; 66 (t) Spencer Grant/PhotoEdit; 67 (tl) Lester Lefkowitz/ Corbis; (c) Jeff Greenberg/PhotoEdit; (b) Bettmann/Corbis; 68 (t) Larry Brownstein/ Ambient Images; (b) Medioimages/ Inmagine; 71 (t) Ansel Adams Publishing Rights Trust/Corbis; 79 (t) The Bancroft Library/ University of California/ Berkeley; 82 (c) Photodisc Red/Getty Images; (bg) C. Moore/Corbis; 83 (t) The Image Bank/ Getty Images; (c) Douglas Slone/Corbis; 84 (t), (bg) Stone/Getty Images; (c) Doug Wilson/Corbis; 86 (c) Ed Young/Corbis; (b) Darrel Gulin/Getty Images; 87 (t) Westwood Area Chamber of Congress; 90 (bg) Joseph Sohm; Visions of America/Corbis; 92 (c) Microzoa/Getty Images; (bg) Jim Wark/Index Stock Imagery; 93 (tr) Digital Vision/Getty Images; (l) Payne Anderson/ Index Stock Imagery; (r) Robert Campbell; Chamois Moon; 95 (t) Topham/The Image Works; 99 (tl), (tr) The Granger Collection/ New York; (c) Corbis; 100 (bg) MacDuff Everton/ Children's Creative Project/ Santa Barbara County Education Office; 102 (c) Hulton Archive/Getty Images; (bl) Joseph Sohm/ChromoSohm Inc./Corbis; 103 (cl) California State Museum Resource Center; (cr) AP/Wide World Photos; 104 (b) Robert Llewellyn; 105 (t) A. Ramey/PhotoEdit; 106 (t) The Image Bank/Getty Images; (c) Stone/Getty Images; 108 (c) Mark E. Gibson Photography; (b) Thomas Hallstein/ Ambient Images; 109 (tr) Mark E. Gibson Photography; (c) Friends of the River; 114 (b) Eliot Cohen; 115 (tl) Blakesley/Photri; (tr) Richard Cummins/Corbis; (c) Theo Allofs/ Corbis; (b) Schwabel/Photo Network; (bg) Maxine Cass.

UNIT 3: 121 (bg) Taxi/Getty Images; 122 (t) Lawrence Migdale; (br) Michael Maloney/ San Francisco Chronicle/Corbis; 123 (tl) K. Hackenberg/zefa/Masterfile; (c) Bob Daemmrich/PhotoEdit; (b) Reuters/Corbis; 124 (b) Ed Kashi/Corbis; 127 (c) Mark E. Gibson/Corbis; 130 (cl) Michael Newman/ PhotoEdit; (cr) Flash! Light/Stock Boston;

(bl) Kelly-Mooney Photography/Corbis; (br) Michelle D. Bridwell/PhotoEdit; 131 (tl) John Coletti/Getty Images; (t) Steve Bourgeois/ Unicorn Stock Photos; (tr) Agence France Presse/Getty Images; (cl) Chronis Jons/Getty Images; (c) Michael Dwyer/Stock/ Boston; (cr), (br) Bob Daemmrich Photography; (bl) Don Smetzer/Getty Images; 133 (tr) David Young-Wolff/PhotoEdit; (l) Stone/Getty Images; (cr) Peter Byron/PhotoEdit; 134 (c) Cesar E. Chavez Foundation; 135 (c) Cesar E. Chavez Foundation; 136 (l) Joe Sohm/Visions of America/PictureQuest; (c) Photodisc Green/Getty Images; 137 (c) Jonathan Nourok/PhotoEdit; (br) David Hiller/Getty Images; 138 (c) Jeff Chiu/AP/Wide World Photos; (b) Marcio Jose Sanchez/AP/Wide World Photos; 139 (cl) Ken Shockley/ City of Fresno City Council; (cr), (br) Courtesy of the Judicial of California, Administrative Office of the Courts; (bl) Fresno City Council; 140 (bl) Dave G. Houser/Corbis; (br) Ken James/ Corbis; 141 (r) Robert W. Ginn/PhotoEdit; 146 (l) Agence France Presse/Getty Images; (r) Samir Mizban/AP/Wide World Photos; 147 (br), (bg) Doug Mills/AP/Wide World Photos; 148 (t) Richard Strauss/Smithsonian Institution/Collection of the Supreme Court of the United States; (b) Chromosohm Media/ Stock Boston; 149 (t) Independence National Historical Park; 152 (b) Bettmann/Corbis; 153 (c), (tl) Ted Streshinsky/Corbis; (tr) Bettmann/Corbis; 156 (t) AFP/Getty Images; (c) Aamir Qureshi/Getty Images; (b) Reuters/ Stefano Rellandini/Corbis; 157 (t) Adam Woolfitt/Corbis; 158 (b) Steve Allen/Getty Images; 159 (cl) International Committee of the Red Cross; (cr) AFP/Getty Images; (b) Paula Bronstein/Stringer/Getty Images; 160 (c) Photri-Microstock; (b) Corbis; 161 (t) NASA (National Space Agency); (c) Mark E. Gibson Photography; (b) Spencer Platt/Getty Images; 162 (b) Elliott Teel Photography/DC Stock Photo; 163 (t) Pool/Getty Images; 166 (c) Digital Vision/Getty Images; (cr) Thinkstock/ Getty Images; 167 (c), (cl) Comstock Images/ Getty Images; (cr) Digital Vision/Getty Images; (b) Western History Collections/ University of Oklahoma Library; 170 (b) Zeum Yerba Buena Gardens; 171 (tl), (b) Carol Simowitz Photography; (tr) Morton Beebe/ Corbis, (c) John Spicer/ Yerba Buena Gardens Festival.

UNIT 4: 177 (bg) Bruce Burkhardt/Corbis; (b) Lawrence Migdale; 178 (br) Grant Heilman Photography; (t) Michael O'Neill/Grant Heilman Photography; 179 (b) Halsey Creative Services/ Inc./StockFood America; (t) James P. Blair/Corbis; 183 (c) Dave G. Houser/Corbis; 188 (b) Emmerich & Webb/ Getty Images; (br) Inmagine/ Comstock; 189 (bg) Monsoon Images/PictureQuest; (fg) Peter Bennett/Ambient Images; (t) Shubroto Chattopadhyay/Index Stock Imagery; 190 (t) Carol Simowitz Photography; (b) Mark E. Gibson Photography; 191 (c) Photodisc Collection/Getty Images; 195 (t) Brown Brothers; 196 (t) Phil Schermeister/Corbis; 198 (t) The Granger Collection/ New York; 199 (r) Myrleen Ferguson Cate/PhotoEdit; (bg) The Granger Collection/ New York; 200 (tl), (c), (bl), (br) David Barker/ Ohio Historical Society; (tr) Susan Van Etten/ PhotoEdit; 201 (r) Nebraska State Historical Society Photograph Collections; (l) The Mariners' Museum/Corbis; 202 (c) Corbis; 203 (fg) Arthur C. Smith/ III/Grant Heilman Photography; (c) Dede Gilman/Unicorn Stock Photos; (bg) Photri-Microstock; 204 (b) Alan Pitcairn/Grant Heilman Photography; 205 (br) Arthur C. Smith/ III/Grant Heilman Photography; (cl) Fernando Bueno/Getty Images; (tr) Pictor Images/Imagestate; (bl) John Colwell/Grant Heilman Photography; (bg) Photri-Microstock; 206 (t), (b) Norris Blake/Visuals Unlimited; 207 (t) National Weather Service/ NOAA; 210 (b) The Edible Schoolyard; (t) Thomas Heinser/Chez Panisse; 211 (t), (b) The Edible Schoolyard; 212 (bg) John Elk/ III/Ambient Images; 213 (t) Bob Fitch/Take Stock; (b) Dave G. Houser/ Corbis; (bg) John Elk III/Ambient Images; 214 (l) Jonathan Nourok; (r) Richard T. Nowitz/Corbis; 216 (bl) Stone/Getty Images; (br) David Young-Wolff/PhotoEdit; (bg) Stone+/Getty Images; 217 (tl) Ryan McVay/ Getty Images; (t) Taxi/Getty Images; 219 (tr) United States Department of Agriculture; (cl) Comstock Images/Getty Images; (cr) Kirk Weddle/Getty Images; 220 (b) Vince Bucci/ Getty Images; 221 (tl) Bob Fitch/Take Stock; (tr) Library of Congress; (c) George Ballis/ Take Stock.

UNIT 5: 233 (br) Lawrence Migdale; (bg) Stone/Getty Images; 234 (t) Spencer Grant/ PhotoEdit; (br) Richard Klune/Corbis; 235 (tl) Photographer's Choice/Getty Images; (c) Coco McCoy/Rainbow; 236 (b) Ralph Epstein/ PhotoEdit; 239 (c) David Young-Wolff/ PhotoEdit; 247 (t) Mark Richards/PhotoEdit; (cr), (br) David Nufer Photography; (bl) Ariel Skelley/Corbis; 248 (c) David Nufer Photography; 249 (r) Charles Gupton/Corbis; (l) David Nufer Photography; 250 (tr), (cl), (c), (cr), (r), Bell Sports, Inc.; 252 (b) David Young-Wolff/PhotoEdit; 254 (b) Associated Press; 255 (fg), (tl), (tr), (cl) Levi Strauss & Co.; 256 (c) David Young-Wolff/PhotoEdit; 257 (cl) Arthur Thevenart/Corbis; (r) Gary Conner/Index Stock Imagery; 259 (c) Tony Freeman/PhotoEdit; 262 (b) PhotoLink/Getty Images; 264 (t) Fabfoodpix.com; (bl) Private Collection/The Bridgeman Art Library; (b) David Barker/ Ohio Historical Society; (br) The Trustees of The British Museum; 265 (t), (tr), (cl), (b) Federal Reserve Bank of San Francisco; (c), (cr) Ira & Larry Goldberg Coins & Collectibles; 266 (t) Smithsonian Institution National Numismatic Collection; (cl), (cr) Smithsonian Institution National Numismatic Collection; (b) Corbis; (br) Institute Monetaire European/Corbis; 269 (t) Dusko Despotovic/Corbis; (c) AP/Wide World Photos; (bl), (b) California Raisin Marketing Board; 270 (c) Photolibrary.com pty.ltd/Index Stock Imagery; 274 (c) Taxi/Getty Images; (cr) Stone/Getty Images; 275 (b) Bettmann/ Corbis; (cl) Ephraim Ben-Shimon/Corbis; (c) Jack Hollingsworth/Getty Images; (cr) Hoby Finn/Getty Images; 276 (fg) Martin Rogers/ Corbis; 277 (bg) Bonnie Kamin/PhotoEdit; 282 (b) Justin Sullivan/Getty Images; 283 (tl) Steve Bein/Corbis; (t) Tim Davis/Corbis; (tr) Port of Oakland; (bg) Robert Campbell/ Chamois Moon.

UNIT 6: 289 (tl) Jose Carillo/PhotoEdit; (tr) Bob Daemmrich/PhotoEdit; (c) James Shaffer/PhotoEdit; (cr) Jonathan Nourok/ PhotoEdit; (bl), (b) Lawrence Migdale; 290 (t) Larry W. Smith/Getty Images; (br) Raymond Gehman/Corbis; 291 (tl) Photo Edit; (tr) NASA; (c) Taxi/Getty Images; (b) George Disario/Corbis; 293 (b) Bettmann/Corbis; 295 (c) The Granger Collection/ New York; 298 (b) Bettmann/Corbis; 299 (cl) National Portrait Gallery/ Smithsonian Institution/Art Resource/ NY; (cr) Bettmann/Corbis; (b) U.S. Department of the Interior/ National Park Service/ Edison National Historic Site; 300 (t) The Granger Collection/ New York; (br) Erich Lessing/Art Resource, NY; 301 (c) Hulton Archive/Getty Images; (bl) Jane Grushow/Grant Heilman Photography; (br) National Portrait Gallery/Smithsonian Institution/Art Resource,NY; 302 (t), (b) The Granger Collection/ New York; (c) Ted Spiegel/Corbis; 303 (t) Bettmann/Corbis; 304 (b) National Museum of American History/ Smithsonian Institution/Behring Center; 305 (t) National Portrait Gallery/ Smithsonian Institution/Art Resource/ NY; (c), (b) The Granger Collection/ New York; 306 (c) Denis Poroy/AP/Wide World Photos; (b) Natalie Rimmer/ UCP/ Lincoln Middle School; 307 (t) Jeff Greenberg/PhotoEdit; (b) Laima Druskis/Jeroboam; 308 (b) Hulton Archive/ Getty Images; 309 (t) Bettmann/Corbis; 310 (b) Time Life Pictures/Getty Images; 311 (t) AP/Wide World Photos; 314 (bl) Jeff Greenberg/PhotoEdit; 315 (t) Tim Roske/AP/ Wide World Photos; (br) Myrleen Ferguson Cate/PhotoEdit; 316 (c) Chris Bacon/AP/ Wide World Photos; (b) World Peace Project For Children/ Mr. Masahiro Sasaki; 317 (c) David Young-Wolff/PhotoEdit; (b) Damian Dovarganes/AP/Wide World Photos; 318 (b) Mark Peterson/Corbis; 319 (tl) David Young-Wolff/PhotoEdit; 320 (b) Time Life Pictures/ Getty Images; 321 (tl) Bettmann/Corbis; (tr) Bachrach/Getty Images; (cl) Time Life Pictures/Getty Images; 322 (bl) NASA; 323 (t) Reuters/Corbis; 324 (c) Time Life Pictures/ Getty Images; (cr) Royalty-Free/Corbis; 325 (cr) Time Life Pictures/Getty Images; 330 (l) Museum of the City of New York/Corbis; (cl), (cr), (r) The Granger Collection, New York; (bg) Paul A. Souders/Corbis; 331 (tl), (t) Mt. Rushmore/National Park Service; (tr) Lionel Green/Hulton/Archive Photos/Getty Images.

REFERENCE:

All other photos from Harcourt School Photo Library and Photographers: Ken Kinzie, April Riehm and Doug Dukane.

California
History–Social Science
Standards and
Analysis Skills

History-Social Science Content Standards
People Who Make a Difference

Students in grade two explore the lives of actual people who make a difference in their everyday lives and learn the stories of extraordinary people from history whose achievements have touched them, directly or indirectly. The study of contemporary people who supply goods and services aids in understanding the complex interdependence in our free-market system.

2.1 Students differentiate between things that happened long ago and things that happened yesterday.

2.1.1 Trace the history of a family through the use of primary and secondary sources, including artifacts, photographs, interviews, and documents.

2.1.2 Compare and contrast their daily lives with those of their parents, grandparents, and/or guardians.

2.1.3 Place important events in their lives in the order in which they occurred (e.g., on a time line or storyboard).

2.2 Students demonstrate map skills by describing the absolute and relative locations of people, places, and environments.

2.2.1 Locate on a simple letter-number grid system the specific locations and geographic features in their neighborhood or community (e.g., map of the classroom, the school).

2.2.2 Label from memory a simple map of the North American continent, including the countries, oceans, Great Lakes, major rivers, and mountain ranges. Identify the essential map elements: title, legend, directional indicator, scale, and date.

2.2.3 Locate on a map where their ancestors live(d), telling when the family moved to the local community and how and why they made the trip.

2.2.4 Compare and contrast basic land use in urban, suburban, and rural environments in California.

2.3 Students explain governmental institutions and practices in the United States and other countries.

2.3.1 Explain how the United States and other countries make laws, carry out laws, determine whether laws have been violated, and punish wrongdoers.

2.3.2 Describe the ways in which groups and nations interact with one another to try to resolve problems in such areas as trade, cultural contacts, treaties, diplomacy, and military force.

2.4 Students understand basic economic concepts and their individual roles in the economy and demonstrate basic economic reasoning skills.

2.4.1 Describe food production and consumption long ago and today, including the roles of farmers, processors, distributors, weather, and land and water resources.

2.4.2 Understand the role and interdependence of buyers (consumers) and sellers (producers) of goods and services.

2.4.3 Understand how limits on resources affect production and consumption (what to produce and what to consume).

2.5 Students understand the importance of individual action and character and explain how heroes from long ago and the recent past have made a difference in others' lives (e.g., from biographies of Abraham Lincoln, Louis Pasteur, Sitting Bull, George Washington Carver, Marie Curie, Albert Einstein, Golda Meir, Jackie Robinson, Sally Ride).

History-Social Science Content Standards

Historical and Social Sciences Analysis Skills

The intellectual skills noted below are to be learned through, and applied to, the content standards for kindergarten through grade five. They are to be assessed *only in conjunction* with the content standards in kindergarten through grade five.

In addition to the standards for kindergarten through grade five, students demonstrate the following intellectual, reasoning, reflection, and research skills:

Chronological and Spatial Thinking

1. Students place key events and people of the historical era they are studying in a chronological sequence and within a spatial context; they interpret time lines.

2. Students correctly apply terms related to time, including *past, present, future, decade, century,* and *generation.*

3. Students explain how the present is connected to the past, identifying both similarities and differences between the two, and how some things change over time and some things stay the same.

4. Students use map and globe skills to determine the absolute locations of places and interpret information available through a map's or globe's legend, scale, and symbolic representations.

5. Students judge the significance of the relative location of a place (e.g., proximity to a harbor, on trade routes) and analyze how relative advantages or disadvantages can change over time.

Research, Evidence, and Point of View

1. Students differentiate between primary and secondary sources.

2. Students pose relevant questions about events they encounter in historical documents, eyewitness accounts, oral histories, letters, diaries, artifacts, photographs, maps, artworks, and architecture.

3. Students distinguish fact from fiction by comparing documentary sources on historical figures and events with fictionalized characters and events.

Historical Interpretation

1. Students summarize the key events of the era they are studying and explain the historical contexts of those events.

2. Students identify the human and physical characteristics of the places they are studying and explain how those features form the unique character of those places.

3. Students identify and interpret the multiple causes and effects of historical events.

4. Students conduct cost-benefit analyses of historical and current events.